THE FULLERTON HOTEL
CapitaLand

PSA

CLEARANCE SALE!

12

POLICE

織雲潮劇團

開工大吉

MUAR'S
OTAH
特制
手工肉丸

SOME HAUNTED SPACES IN SINGAPORE

Marcel Jäggi, Charlotte Malterre-Barthes

Edition Patrick Frey
N° 271

CONTENTS

Preface by Mary-Ann Ray

SPOOK SPACE

With my limited knowledge of—but expansive fascination with—Singapore's Housing & Development Board (HDB) buildings, it has always been disturbing and intriguing to know that each dwelling has lurking at its very core a space of terror, a dark side, a reminder of our mortality: that space being the bomb shelter as required by Singaporean law to be provided to every subsidized household.

Marcel Jäggi and Charlotte Malterre-Barthes's studies of *Haunted Spaces in Singapore* reminded me of this, and of Eric Khoo's film *12 Storeys*. In the film, a series of narratives are set within the twelve floors of an average Singaporean HDB. In the opening establishing shot, one resident jumps to his death from the twelfth floor, thumping down onto the concrete below. This sets off one of the stories, titled "Spirit," in which the ghost of that young man goes on to permeate—to haunt—the film, the characters, the narratives and the physical space of the HDB. The stories told in *12 Storeys* revolve around daily life in the HDB and its inhabitants, who are under siege from the effects of rapid urbanization, which at their best produce banality and ennui and at their worst cause alienation and disorientation, or as the authors describe it: "the loss of memory, disappearance of reference points, and the fading sense of belonging." The authors identify the belief in ghosts as a "resistance mechanism" to help counter such ill effects.

In Rem Koolhaas's musing on Coney Island in *Delirious New York*, he remarks that "instead of suspension of urban pressure"—as one might assume an amusement park would provide—"it offers intensification."[1] So, in the early days at the Island, there were stagings of six or seven disaster spectacles every day. These included "a Dreamland extravaganza called 'Fighting the Flames,'" which "featured six-story tenement buildings and two thousand performers, and the crowd watching the firemen as part of the production was hardly distinguishable from the paying audience."[2] Koolhaas proposed that by being immersed in intensifications of disasters that paralleled the real ones taking place in the real city, it made it easier to live with the everyday pressures and in fact produced a kind of antidote or antibody for coping. In the case of Coney Island, these were clearly constructed productions. In the case of the haunted spaces of Singapore, they are a kind of mash-up of real stories, myths and beliefs. But in both cases, it points us toward an idea that within human nature there exists a kind of necessity for the presence of horror and reminders of death and danger in our daily lives.

From Singapore's haunted city, to Coney Island's frightful spectacles, my mind then wandered to Ancient Rome—one of my old haunts. The necessity for haunted and horrific space is not confined to contemporary conditions or eastern culture. In Joseph Rykwert's brilliant book *The Idea of a Town*, he goes into great depth describing the origin myths and rituals of Roman cities.[3] Cities, and especially Rome itself, are steeped in superstition and the presence of otherworldly spirits. In Ancient Rome, lurking behind rational urban planning devices such as the *castrum* grid and the *cardus* and *decumaus*, were more non-empirical and mythic methods that included augury and animal haruspicy—taking cues from the flight patterns of birds or from their livers. The center of the city was occupied by a pit known as the *mundus*. The beginning of the survey established the layout of the urban configuration. It was covered by the *lapis niger*—a black stone cap—and was said to be "the mouth of hell." One day each year, the cap was removed and the evil spirits from the underworld were said to roam the city, and all manner of mayhem might break loose. This ritual seems to have served some collective urban social need that had the positive effect of making it easier to dwell within the city for the remainder of the year.

So, while "spook space" is a deeply human necessity existing throughout time and place, the work of *Some Haunted Spaces in Singapore* holds an especially relevant message for us as contemporary global urban residents of the Anthropocene. The authors describe their narratives of the spooked spaces of Singapore "as an attempt to see beyond physical realities." While the book does an amazing job of this, it also has a fascinating and substantial side effect of making a convincing case for the necessity of physical spaces to exist as vessels for spirits and the spiritual. With rapid urbanization somewhat behind us, we face other potentially more extreme traumas such as the effects of climate change, genetic modification, the dark potentials of artificial intelligence and nuclear annihilation. The authors' rigorous, thorough and poetic documentation and description of the haunted spaces of Singapore should cause us to pause and to realize that we perhaps need to collectively embrace and even promote paradoxes within and between physical space—the city, the monument, the building, the room—and spiritual beliefs, superstition and the supernatural. "Spook space" might just get us through the onslaught of things to come.

1 Rem Koolhaas, *Delirious New York: A Retroactive Manifesto for Manhattan* (New York: The Monacelli Press, 2014), 33.

2 Nancy Bentley, *Frantic Panoramas: American Literature and Mass Culture, 1870–1920* (Philadelphia: University of Pennsylvania Press, 2012).

3 Joseph Rykwert, *The Idea of a Town: The Anthropology of Urban Form in Rome, Italy and the Ancient World* (London: Faber and Faber, 2013).

SOME HAUNTED SPACES IN SINGAPORE MAP

CASE STUDIES: 1 AMBER BEACON TOWER 2 SOONG SISTERS HOUSE 3 OLD SIA GROUP SPORTS CLUB 4 WOODY LODGE 5 HAW PAR VILLA 6 HILLVIEW MANSION 7 BISHAN MRT STATION 8 BUKIT BROWN CEMETERY

NON-EXHAUSTIVE LIST: 9 BEDOK RESERVOIR 10 BRADDELL-WESTLAKE SCHOOL 11 CHANGI COMMANDO BARRACKS 12 CHOA CHU KANG CEMETERY 13 DAIRY FARM 14 FORMER CID HEADQUARTERS 15 FLAMINGO VALLEY CONDOS

16 INSTITUTE OF MENTAL HEALTH 17 ISTANA WOODNEUK 18 JURONG CENTRAL PARK 19 KAMPONG LORONG BUANGKOK 20 KERAMAT BUKIT KASITA 21 LABRADOR PARK 22 MATILDA HOUSE 23 NEE SOON CAMP 24 NEO TIEW ESTATE 25 OLD CHANGI HOSPITAL 26 OLD FORD FACTORY 27 OLD HOUSE AT ALEXANDRA ROAD 28 OLD JOO CHIAT POLICE STATION 29 OLD OPERA ESTATE SCHOOL 30 PULAU TEKONG 31 SEMBAWANG PARK 32 SENTOSA BEACH 33 ST JOHN'S ISLAND 34 TANGLIN HILL BRUNEI HOSTEL 35 THE RED HOUSE 36 THOMSON SECONDARY SCHOOL 37 VIEW ROAD HOSPITAL 38 YISHUN PARK 39 PULAU HANTU BESAR / PULAU HANTU KECIL

1

AMBER BEACON TOWER

1°17'52" N 103°54'21" E

920 EAST COAST PARKWAY, SINGAPORE

BUILT IN 1979

COMMISSIONER: MARITIME AND PORT AUTHORITY

1 AMBER BEACON TOWER 2 EAST COAST PARK 3 EAST COAST PARKWAY (ECP)
4 KATONG 5 STRAITS OF SINGAPORE

This peculiar lighthouse is a well-known haunted architectural object facing the Straits of Singapore. The beacon was the site of a mysterious murder in the 1990s. Sitting and chatting on the stairs at night, a couple were attacked and the woman stabbed to death. The murderers are still at large. Since then, the lighthouse has been said to be haunted. Also known as the Yellow Tower, it is listed by the Marine and Port Authorities of Singapore (MPA) as the "East Control" reporting station, helping ships to navigate through the Straits. The amber light beams from the top of the tower. Constructed in 1979, the bright-yellow mosaic-tiled cylinder stands alone, at the limits of the park, on the beach, near Carpark C. On a concrete-core construction, a staircase with metallic railings spirals up to an accessible terrace. It is there that people claim to have spotted the ghost of the murdered girl. There is a wealth of do-it-yourself, grassroots investigations by various groups or individuals searching for signs of the ghost. The factual and dramatic aspect of the case, placing Amber Beacon as a murder scene, makes it a perfect site for ghost-hunters, spiritual daredevils, and believers in the afterlife. Revealing of the huge interest Singaporeans take in spiritual matters and ghosts, Amber Beacon stands as an iconic object: "ghost-chasing for beginners." What campers and ghost-hunters might not be aware of is that the Yellow Tower is built on reclaimed land. From the 1960s till the 1980s, entire hills of the island's central areas were leveled and the earth dumped in the sea to expand Singapore's territory, here at East Coast Park. While the soil is ancient, it is nevertheless perceived as a new piece of land, devoid of history. The past is made undetectable by reclamation processes. Yet, with time, new stories arise, and the ghostly encounters at Amber Beacon point to spiritual beliefs as one of the strongest mechanisms of appropriation and collective identity building.

Couple stabbed at beacon tower in East Coast Park

Woman dies after sudden attack by two unknown men while man is warded

By Foo Siang Luen

MYSTERY surrounds the stabbing of a couple at a beacon tower in the East Coast Park on Tuesday night.

Miss Tan Ah Hong, 21, died soon after she and a friend, Mr James Soh Fook Leong, 22, were attacked from behind by two unknown men as they sat and chatted on the spiral staircase of Amber Beacon at about 10.30 pm.

The beacon, near Parkland Golf Driving Range, is a device which sends out light signals to ships, warning them that they are close to shore.

Mr Soh is a third-year electronics engineering student at the Ngee Ann Polytechnic while Miss Tan helped her father in his vegetable business.

Police said the two men had earlier walked past Miss Tan and Mr Soh on their way to the top of the tower. About 15 minutes later, the men came down and attacked the couple.

The injured couple staggered to the nearby Singa Inn Seafood Restaurant where Miss Tan collapsed at the back entrance while Mr Soh, his shirt covered with blood, slumped onto a table.

Police arrived and found Miss Tan dead with a stab wound on the left of the neck, below the ear.

Mr Soh, who had a stab wound on his back, was sent to the Singapore General Hospital. He is conscious and his condition is stable.

No weapon was recovered at the scene.

The seemingly senseless attack has baffled Mr Soh's parents. Said his mother, 47, who wanted to be known only as Madam Tan: "I just don't know who would want to do a thing like this. I am sure he has no enemies because he is a very obedient boy and seldom goes out at night."

She said yesterday that her son had left their Sing Avenue home at about 7.30 pm without saying where he was going.

Madam Tan said that as far as she knew, Mr Soh, her only son, did not have a steady girlfriend. "He has many friends but since he is an adult I do not pry into his personal affairs. I have not seen Miss Tan before."

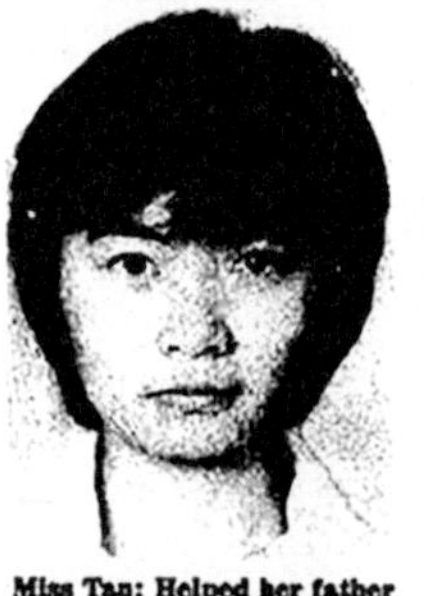

Miss Tan: Helped her father in his vegetable business.

Mr Soh: He is lucky to be alive, said his mother.

She said she was informed of the incident by a staff of the restaurant.

"Fook Leong was conscious when I arrived at the scene. He could not talk but indicated with his hand that he was all right. He still does not know that Miss Tan is dead."

Madam Tan said her son was "lucky to be alive because he is a powerfully-built boy".

Mr Soh's father, who declined to be named, said he found his car, a Subaru, near the scene of the attack.

"My son borrowed my car and his wallet was still inside. As for Miss Tan, I only saw her once in my home a few days ago and Fook Leong said she was an ex-schoolmate."

Miss Tan's family refused to be interviewed.

Amber Beacon, where the stabbings took place on Tuesday night. Arrow shows where the couple were attacked.

"AMBER BEACON, WHERE THE STABBINGS TOOK PLACE ON TUESDAY NIGHT. ARROW SHOWS WHERE THE COUPLE WAS ATTACKED." (SOURCE: *THE STRAITS TIMES*, MAY 17, 1990)

Murdered girl's family makes second appeal

Uneasy nights for mother, sisters as they wait for news

THE family of murder victim Kelly Tan Ah Hong has not been able to sleep easy for the past two years.

Her mother, Madam Ong Lye, 42, and her sisters often have nightmares about Kelly's murder at Amber Beacon Tower on May 15, 1990. The tower is near the Singa Inn restaurant at the East Coast Park.

Yesterday Madam Ong, Miss Tan's elder sister Kwee Mui and their cousin Mr Anthony Tan, 28, made a second appeal for information on the murder.

Miss Tan Kwee Mui, 26, said: "The last two years have been torture for us, knowing that the person or persons who killed Kelly are still at large. No one can understand the loss we feel. The only consolation we have is the photos of Kelly that we have all over the house."

She and her mother could not hold back their tears at the Police Headquarters yesterday as they talked about Kelly and her unsolved murder.

Miss Tan described her sister as vivacious and the favourite in the family of seven children. Her sister was always willing to help out with household chores and in the family's vegetable wholesale business, she said.

She also repeated the offer of a $30,000 reward for information leading to the arrest and conviction of Miss Tan's assailants that the family had first made in April.

Miss Kelly Tan: Stabbed from behind at the East Coast Park.

A police spokesman said some people had called about the incident but no one had given them concrete information which would lead to the arrest or conviction of the murderer.

Miss Kelly Tan, then 21, was stabbed to death by one or two assailants while out on a date with ex-schoolmate James Soh at about 10.30 pm.

Mr Soh, then 22, was stabbed in the back but survived the attack. They had both been sitting on the steps of the Amber Beacon Tower when two men attacked them from behind.

The one who attacked Mr Soh had short hair and was about 1.73 m tall. The other had curly black hair and was about 1.67 m tall.

Mr Soh told police the shorter man wore a dark-coloured short-sleeved shirt and dark coloured jeans.

After the attack, the taller man ran towards Singa Inn restaurant while the other attacker headed towards the bird sanctuary at the park.

Police are hoping that customers at the restaurant may have seen the first assailant and might come forward to give information on the murder.

They are asked to call the CID at 222-0000 or the police hotline at 225-0000.

The family's appeal will also be telecast during Crime Watch in Mandarin on Saturday at 10.15 pm on Channel 8, and in English on Sunday at 9.45 pm on Channel 5.

Mr Anthony Tan said: "The family has suffered a lot. Kelly's mother and younger sisters frequently dream of her and even have nightmares about her death.

"Although it has been two years now, the loss remains as great because the men who attacked her and James have not been found."

"MURDERED GIRL'S FAMILY MAKE SECOND APPEAL," (SOURCE: *THE STRAITS TIMES*, JUNE 11, 1992)

AMBER BEACON

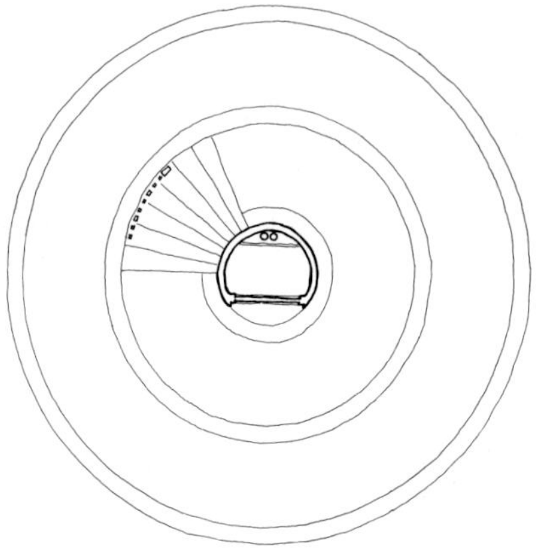

GROUND FLOOR

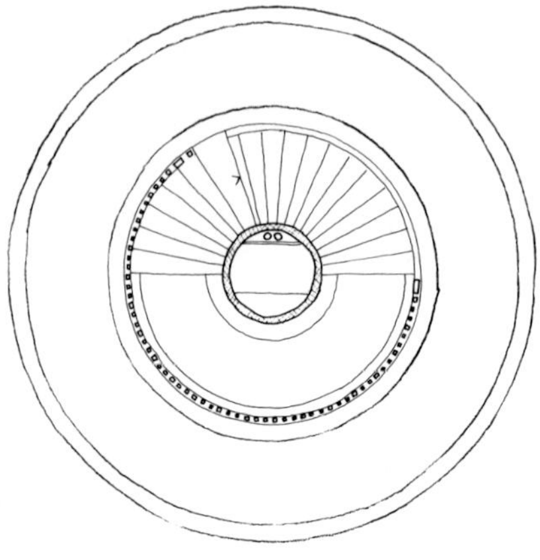

FIRST FLOOR

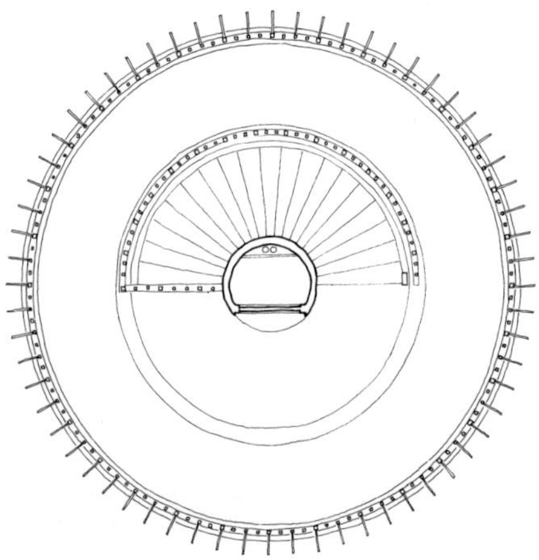

VIEWING TERRACE (THIRD FLOOR)

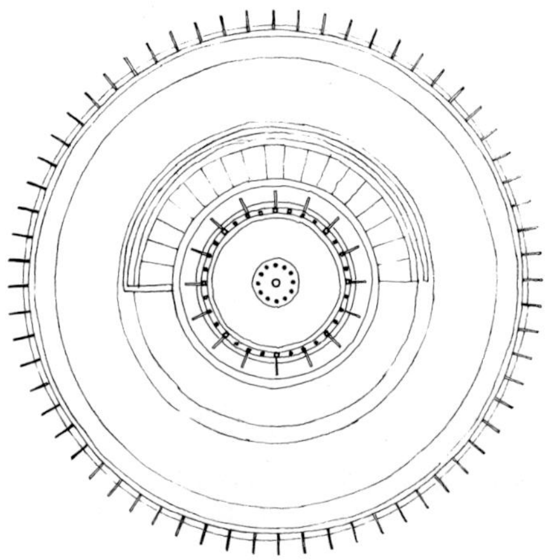

TOP FLOOR WITH BEACON

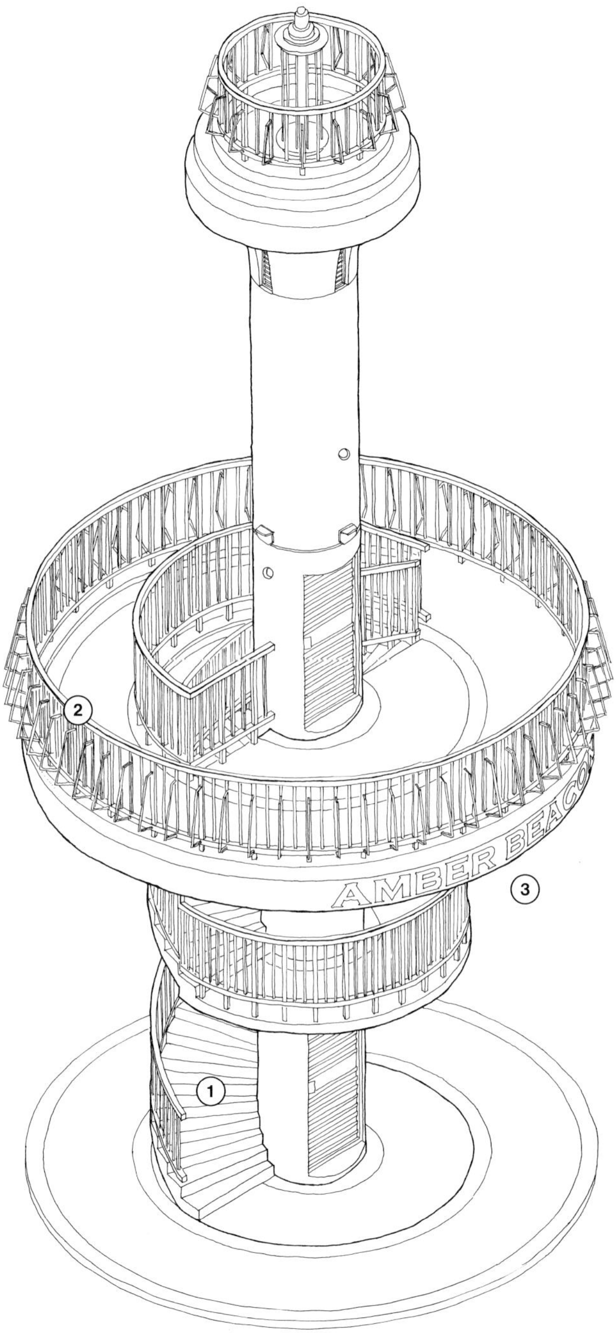

1 CRIME SCENE (MURDER) 2 MESSAGES SCRATCHED IN HANDRAIL 3 ALLEGED SECOND CRIME SCENE (SUICIDE)

BEACON

SOONG SISTERS HOUSE

1°17'56"N 103°50'07"E

25 GRANGE ROAD, SINGAPORE

BUILT IN 1938, LISTED AS A HERITAGE BUILDING SINCE 2008

ARCHITECT: HO KWONG YEW

COMMISSIONER: CHEE GUAN CHIANG

1 OOONG SISTERS HOUSE 2 ORCHARD ROAD 3 NGEE ANN CITY 4 LEONIE HILL

Every Singaporean knows that Soong Sisters House, 25 Grange Road, is haunted. Some say people died when one of the buildings on the compound burned down; some have heard voices, and some have seen shapes on the verandas. Generations of teenagers have trespassed there at night to test their courage. The beautiful, now seemingly abandoned Art Deco villa is on a small hill off Orchard Road, hidden by dark, lush vegetation, malls glowing in the near distance, condominiums towering over the building. Built in 1938 for Chee Guan Chiang, heir of a Chinese family from Malacca (Malaysia), by the architect Ho Kwong Yew, it replaced a previous house, the Moss Bank. The building is part of an original development of four houses, of which one is now a furniture shop down the street, the second a ruin, while the third was sold and demolished to make way for one of the Grange Heights condominium towers. From its construction till today, the house saw various occupants, and for some time was even used as a hostel. Because an almost century-old agreement granting right of passage for the owners of each house was challenged in court, legal disputes are ongoing and have spared the house from falling prey to urban development. The resulting lack of maintenance accelerated decay, catalysing the public perception of "a haunted house." The building was granted protection in 2008 by the Conservation Department of the URA (Urban Redevelopment Authority). In 2016, unable to sell the plot for an estimated S$23 million, current owner Lee Tat Development sued Grange Heights for lost opportunity damages. Save for a family of caretakers and an impressive number of pots, the house remains unoccupied. Christened "Soong Sisters House" by ghost-hunters Asia Paranormal Investigators, a reference to the three sisters who married into one of China's most powerful families, the nickname has stuck. With a distinct architectural style, rounded terraces and balconies, the building stands witness to a long-gone colonial heyday, a tiny structure sitting on prime land, overshadowed by the forty-storey residential towers on adjacent plots. On an island where speculation-driven fast-paced growth tends to tear up the urban fabric, Soong Sisters House is an exception, at odds with its surroundings and its time.

THE SUNDAY TIMES

The Leading Sunday Newspaper In Malaya.

No. 324 — Sunday, March 6, 1938 — Price 10 cents

New Architecture In Singapore

INDICATING a departure from the old style of domestic architecture in Malaya are the modern, flat-roofed reinforced concrete, Singapore homes.

The old, classical style of home appears to be dying, giving way to a type promising to be more suitable for the tropics.

The greater projection of roof giving more shadow lends coolness, and architects agree that room planning is easier when they haven't got to worry about a tiled roof.

Air conditioning, which is bound to come in the future as soon as plants are more moderately priced, can be more easily applied to this type of building, architects say.

Bedrooms can be air-conditioned much more easily in these houses than in the old type with open rooms, and mosquito nets can be dispensed with.

HOW Mr. Chee Guan Chiang's present residence in Grange Road looks at ground level.

MR. M. E. ISAAC'S residence in Meyer Road.

THE NEW RESIDENCE under construction for Mr. Chee Guan Chiang in Grange Road.

SPACIOUS AND AIRY: Mr. L. Langdon Williams' residence off the Singapore Golf Course road

ANOTHER VIEW of Mr. L. Langdon Williams' residence.

The Sunday Times

THE HOUSE IS MENTIONED IN AN ARTICLE ON "NEW ARCHITECTURE IN SINGAPORE" AS THE "NEW RESIDENCE UNDER CONSTRUCTION FOR MR. CHEE GUAN CHIANG IN GRANGE ROAD." (SOURCE: *THE SUNDAY TIMES*, MARCH 6, 1938)

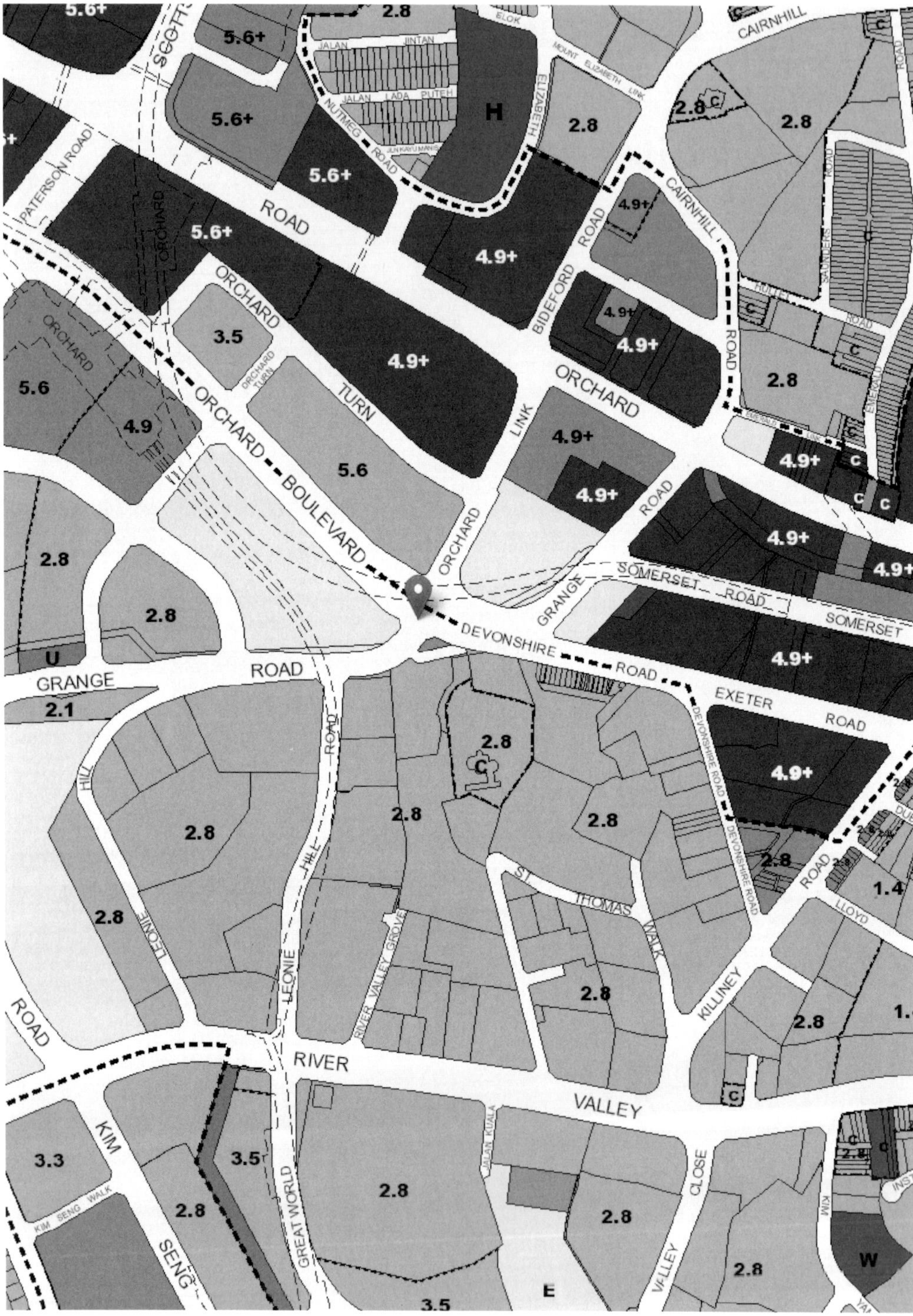

THE HOUSE STANDS IN A RESIDENTIAL ZONE WITH A PERMISSABLE PLOT RATIO OF 2.8 AS PER LATEST MASTER PLAN (SOURCE: URBAN REDEVELOPMENT AUTHORITY AND PHYSICAL PLANNING, 2015)

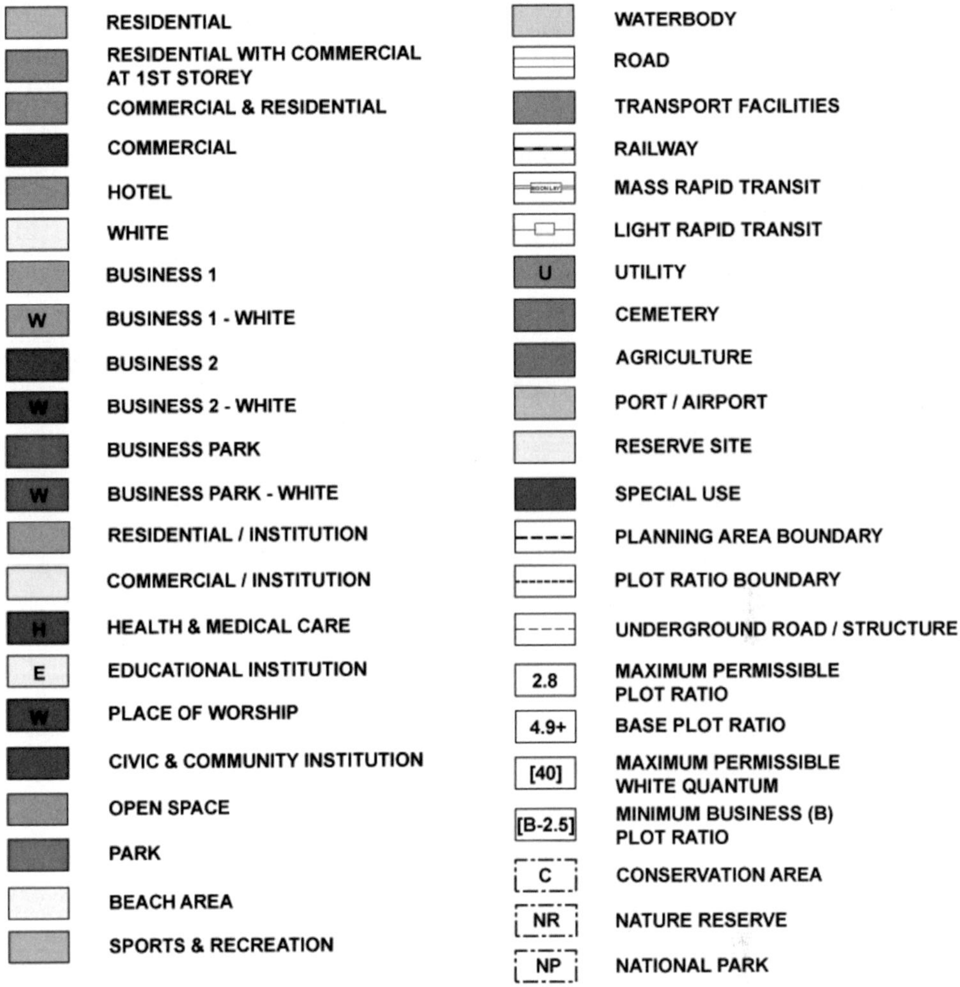

MASTER PLAN LEGEND (SOURCE: URBAN REDEVELOPMENT AUTHORITY AND PHYSICAL PLANNING, 2015)

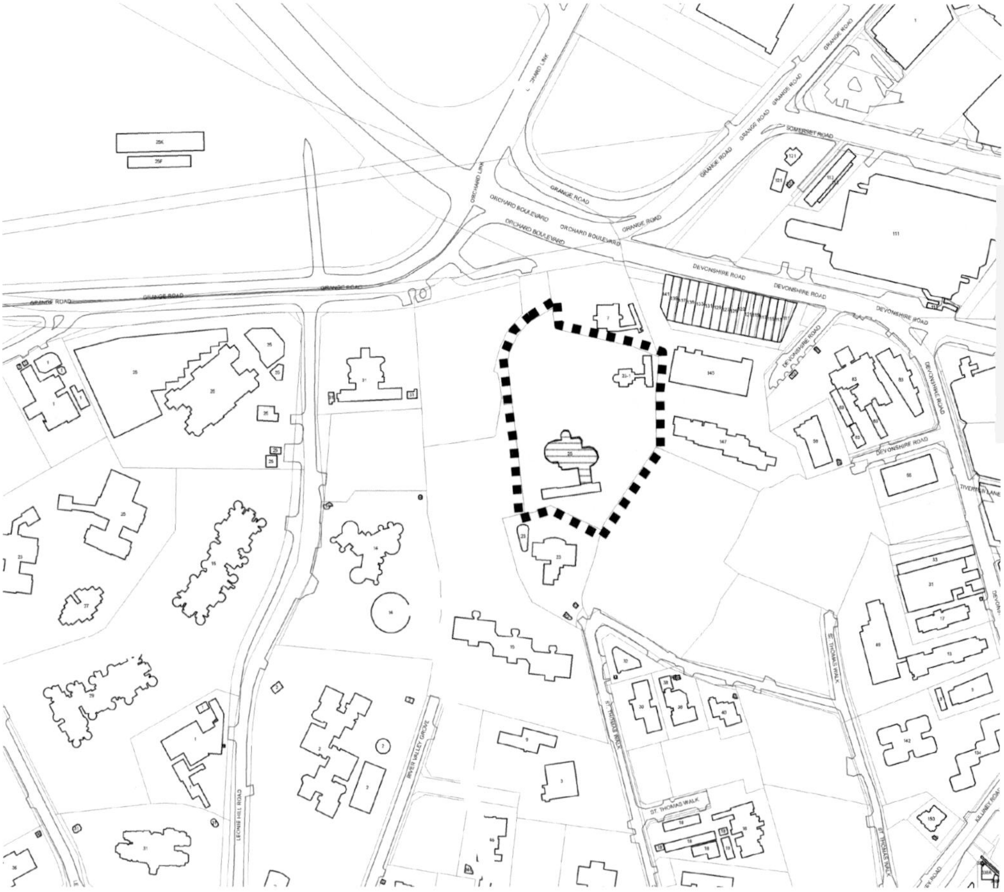

CONSERVATION PLAN OF THE HOUSE AND OF THE BOUNDARIES OF THE GAZETTED AREA AT 25 GRANGE ROAD (SOURCE: URBAN REDEVELOPMENT AUTHORITY AND PHYSICAL PLANNING, 2008)

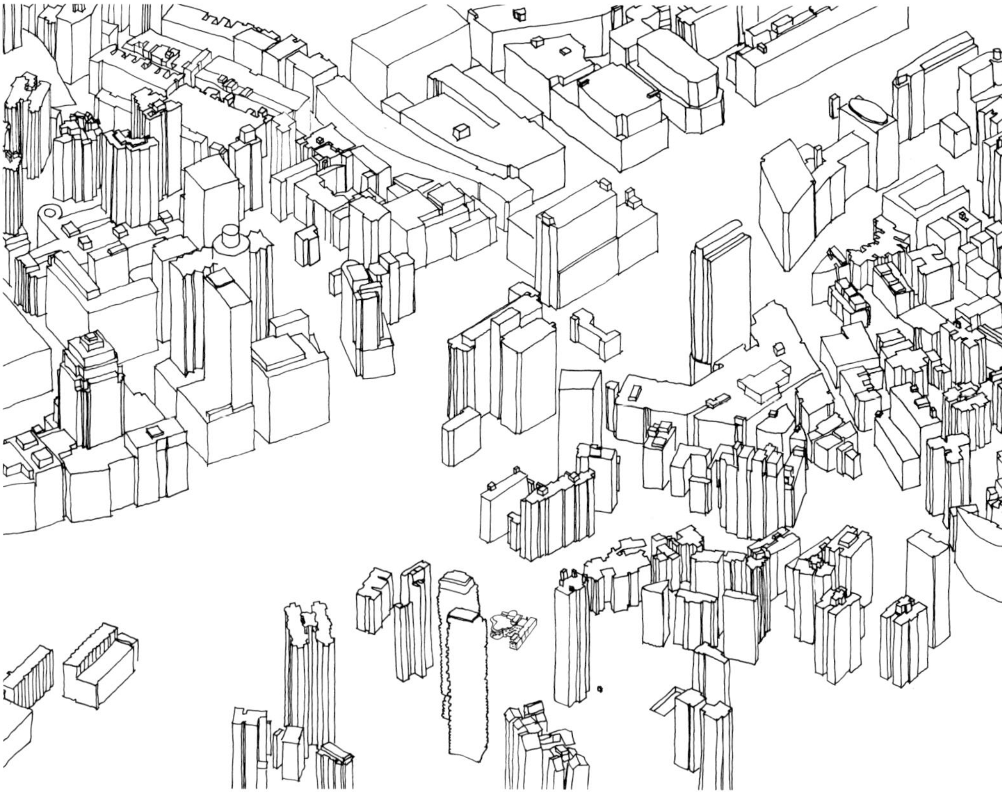

CONTEXT OF CONTRASTS—SURROUNDED BY HIGH-RISE CONDOMINIUMS AND LARGE SHOPPING MALLS, THE HOUSE STANDS ON PRIME REAL ESTATE LAND, BOTH A PROVOCATION AND A WITNESS

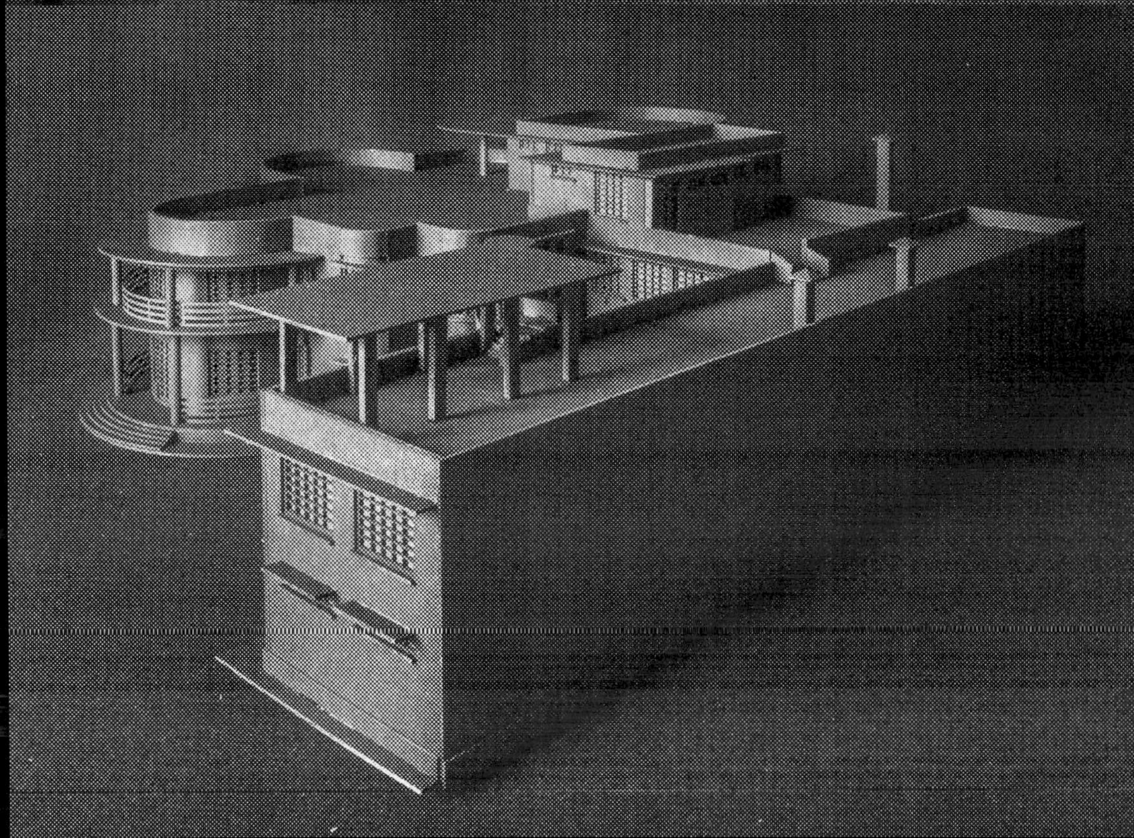

3

OLD SIA GROUP SPORTS CLUB

1°23'28" N 103°58'45" E

24 TURNHOUSE ROAD, SINGAPORE

BUILT IN 1982, CLOSED IN 2006

COMMISSIONER: SINGAPORE AIRLINES (SIA) GROUP

1 OLD SIA SPORTS CLUB 2 OLD CHANGI HOSPITAL 3 BEACH 4 FORMER ARMY BARRACKS 5 STRAITS OF JOHOR

A pedestrian bridge raised over an empty carpark leads occasional sightseers to the main entrance of the former Singapore Airlines (SIA) Group Sports and Recreation Club, close to Changi Village. The gates are locked and the *Bismillah* sign nailed to the door should discourage entry, implying the presence of ghosts. Inside, the wire traps possibly placed there by security guards are broken—indicating uninvited guests. Yet the sports club is abandoned; only the Komodo dragons in the pool and the black cats in the garden inhabit this quiet place. Completed in October 1982, the now vacant state property lies silent, somewhat neglected in a far-off part of Singapore's domestic hinterland, in an area where many buildings of the former Royal Air Force Changi Air Base can be found. Facing the southern tip of the Malaysian Sultanate of Johor, a short distance from the sea, the neighborhood is infamous. During the Japanese occupation in World War II, thousands of Singaporean Chinese were tortured and killed here by the

Japanese Imperial Army in what is known as the "Sook Ching massacre." Locals have considered the entire Changi area, with its beaches, old army camps, and former commando barracks, to be haunted ever since. Unsurprisingly, numerous ghost stories exist about the place, from overheard screams to coastal waters turning red from the victims' blood. Additionally, where the sports club's outdoor tennis and basketball courts now are, was previously the site of the formerly adjacent Changi Hospital's infirmary and morgue. In stark contrast to the site's cruel past, the sports club is a picturesque example of 1980s tropical modernist architecture. The building's award-winning design is characterized by expressive forms: dome-shaped lobby, sloping roofs, wide eaves, mushroom pillars and cantilevered balconies clad in white ceramic tiles. Unsurprisingly, the impressive seven-lane Olympic-size swimming pool served as the club's key facility, around which other spaces, such as the viewing terrace, are placed. The club pampered its members, the SIA staff: the building had food and beverage stalls, a sports gym, library and meeting rooms, a salon, a one-armed bandit and electronic games, TVs, darts and billiards rooms. At a time when many larger organizations were investing in comparable leisure spaces, membership of the 2.68-hectare, $11-million club also meant social prestige. Conceived as a "chalet," the complex was presented as a welcome escape from Singapore's dense center and claustrophobic urbanization. Membership fell drastically in the first years of operations, from a few thousands to twelve hundred. Increased membership fees, remoteness, and lack of transportation were among the precipitating factors—possibly with the allegedly coinciding existence of the other world's presence. A perfectly fine building, it became quickly unfashionable for the SIA sports club—who eventually moved closer to the airport in 2006, literally abandoning the clubhouse at Turnhouse Road. The new clubhouse

THE CLUB IN THE 1980s, WITH THE SINGAPORE AIRLINES LOGO EMBLAZONING ITS TILED FACADE (SOURCE: SINGAPORE TOURIST PROMOTION BOARD)

DURING THEIR OCCUPATION OF THE ISLAND IN 1942, JAPANESE TROOPS PURGED “ANTI-JAPANESE” CITIZENS AMONG THE CHINESE COMMUNITY OF SINGAPORE, SORTING AND LINING UP SUSPECTED MEN WHO WERE EXECUTED—OPERATION *SOOK CHING* (CHINESE FOR “PURGE THROUGH CLEANSING”). THE BEACH OF CHANGI, NEAR THE SIA COMPLEX, IS ONE OF THE MASSACRE SITES (SOURCE: NATIONAL LIBRARY SINGAPORE)

with its generic architecture is conceived as a Club Med of sorts, hosting weddings and spa retreats. The old club's specific and contextual architecture became demoded, thus falling victim to the mechanisms of obsolescence valid all across the island that declare a building's life span to be thirty years. Today, there is a minimum maintenance effort to preserve the building's surface and long-term value. The complex remains unused, save for occasional happenings such as art video shoots or boutique open-air music festivals, playing with the place's seclusion and haunted image. While the Urban Redevelopment Authority of Singapore (URA) is looking for new tenants, the future of the old clubhouse is uncertain. Although the ghosts' presence was only a side story in this development at first, this aspect is by now the most enduring. While the alleged presence of spirits did not disturb the erection of the complex in the first place, the building's public perception of being haunted increased due to its abandonment and the visual signs of slow decay. To what extend this plays a role in sparing the space from further development is unclear —however, ghost stories are regularly used to chase unwelcome buyers away. Following the same logic, they are also instrumentalized to reduce real estate prices in other cases. In a superstitious place like Singapore, implying that a place is haunted affects a person's willingness to invest in it or not, depending on how believable the ghost story is. Thus, one must therefore ask who placed the *Bismillah* sign on the door?

VIEWS OF THE ROYAL AIR FORCE AIRMEN'S SWIMMING POOL (SOURCE: ANDY MACDONALD, 1967)

Anyone for tennis?

The most striking illustration of the SIA Group's interest in the health and welfare of its staff is the Changi Sports Complex being built for members of the SIA Group Sports & Recreation Club. When completed later this year, at a cost of $11 million, the complex will be one of the most comprehensive and beautiful sporting and recreational facilities in Singapore.

Sited on 2.9 hectares of land facing the sea, the complex is bounded on the north by the Singapore Yacht Club and the sea, on the west by playing fields, on the east by Government holiday bungalows, and on the south by Turnhouse Road (off Netheravon Road).

Chalet-style building

The architecture of the complex is imaginative in concept and bold in design, featuring a four-level chalet-style building with sloping roofs, wide eaves and cantilevered balconies. It has a total covered floor space of approximately 7,000 square metres and a carpark for one hundred cars. An important aspect of the design is the viewing terrace, which links all the sports and recreational areas. A roof deck on the topmost level of one wing offers superb views of the general surroundings, while a viewing balcony overlooks the multi-purpose hall and the four squash courts.

Facilities at the complex include the multi-purpose hall with its three badminton courts; an outdoor multi-purpose court for basketball, netball, sepak takraw and volleyball; three Techtone-surfaced tennis courts and a practice wall; a table tennis room; a fully equipped children's playing area; and an open field for football and hockey. A seven-lane Olympic swimming pool and a children's pool are flanked by a terrace offering a snack kiosk on one side and the four squash courts on the other.

Indoor games and hobbies areas are located in the main building. One airconditioned room houses jackpot and electronic games; other airconditioned areas include the bar and lounge, a reading room, a billiards room with provision for three tables, the television and darts room, a conference room, and the general office.

There will also be a health and fitness club, utilising the latest fitness and exercise equipment, and run by qualified physical fitness instructors. The surroundings of the complex also offer excellent opportunities for such outdoor activities as walking, jogging, cycling, orienteering and roller skating. A sporting goods shop will be set up to look after the equipment needs of members.

Solar water heating

Good food, of course, has not been forgotten, and there will be a restaurant with both Muslim and non-Muslim kitchens.

In keeping with the Government's campaign to save energy, the complex is fitted with a solar hot water system to conserve energy.

Club members, whether working normal office hours or on shift work, will find the complex a place for enjoyment and relaxation at any time.

"THE MOST STRIKING ILLUSTRATION OF THE SIA GROUP'S INTEREST IN THE HEALTH [...] OF ITS STAFF IS THE CHANGI SPORTS COMPLEX" READS AN ADVERTISING ARTICLE TITLED "ANYONE FOR TENNIS?" THE ADVERTISEMENT ARTICLE MENTIONS THE ARCHITECTURE OF THE COMPLEX AS "IMAGINATIVE AND BOLD." (SOURCE: *THE STRAITS TIMES*, ADVERTISEMENT, JUNE 18, 1981)

THE POOL IS SOMETIMES USED FOR PARTIES WHICH ATTRACT YOUTH AND EXPATRIATE CROWDS, OCCUPYING THE SPACE FOR A NIGHT (SOURCE: SUPER 0 SINGAPORE, JANUARY 17, 2015)

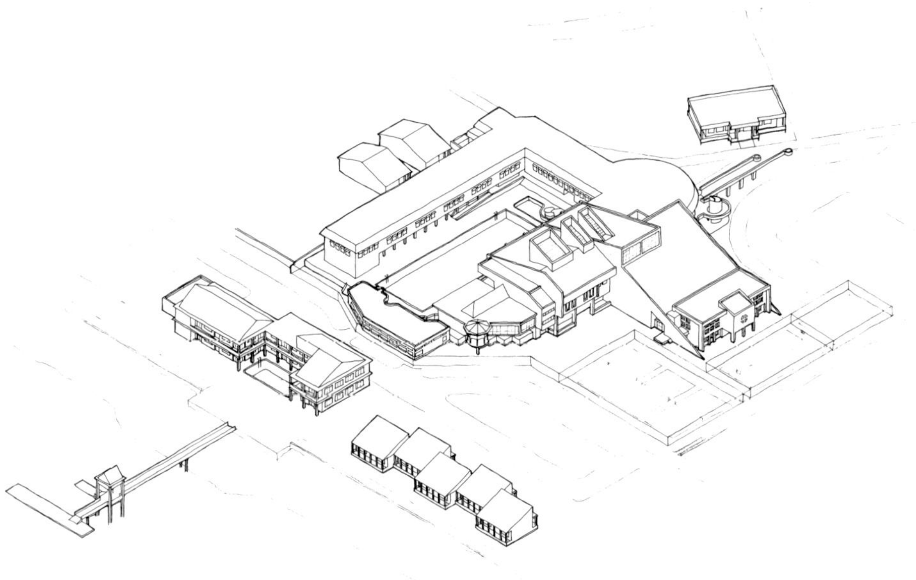

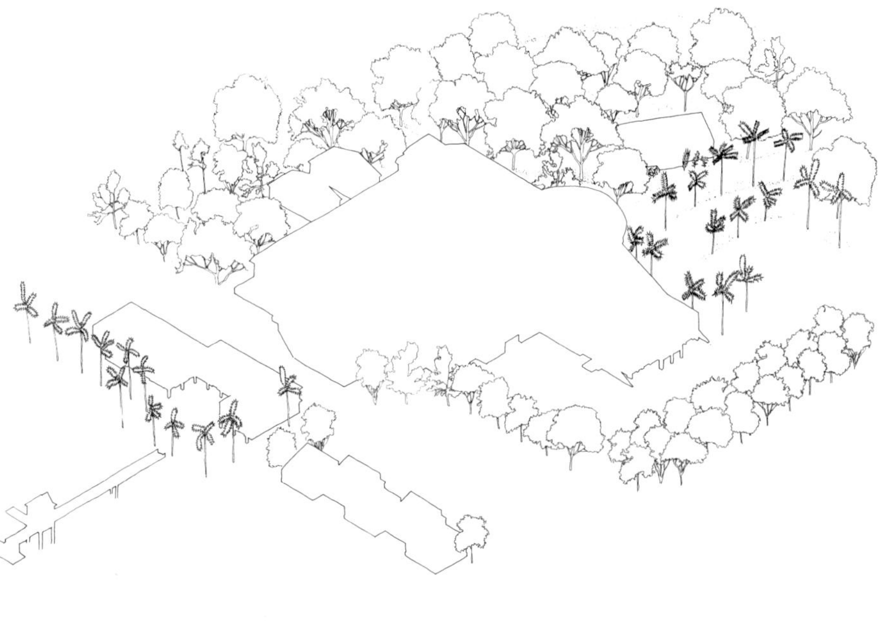

DIRTY AND CLEAN—THE NOW ABANDONED SPORTS CLUB
EMBEDDED IN ITS CAREFULLY MANICURED TROPICAL ENVIRONMENT

WOODY LODGE

1°23'04"N 103°52'52"E

81 BUANGKOK CRESCENT, SINGAPORE

BUILT AS TRAFALGAR HOSPITAL IN THE 1920s, DEMOLISHED IN 2014

COMMISSIONER: BRITISH COLONIAL AUTHORITY

1 WOODY LODGE 2 INSTITUTE OF MENTAL HEALTH 3 KAMPUNG LORONG BUANKOK 4 SUNGEI PUNGGOL

Framed by a large banyan tree and a derelict gondola cabin, Woody Lodge's admission office building was attractive but derelict. Visitors had been received there when entering this eerie place a few years ago—today it is all gone. A state property, the whole site was cleared for the development of Buangkok Square, a mixed-use development including public housing and a neighborhood center currently under construction. Woody Lodge was a care home for destitute persons, housing in its heyday up to 215 elderly male Singaporean Chinese and Indian residents suffering from mental illness. Demolished in 2014, the complex shared the fate of its immediate neighboring buildings along Lorong Buangkok, a former leprosy asylum, and another home for psychiatric patients. Advocated by modern scientific theory, the isolation of persons with mental and infectious diseases was made compulsory during colonial times. The British colonial authorities sealed off this area away from the city center, building several homes for the "dangerously sick" in the 1920s (Trafalgar Hospital). Woody Lodge was established there only in 1986 as a welfare institution which was later relocated to a so-called "activity hub" nearby. The "Sun Love Home for the Intellectually Infirm" ("Surya Home") moved in for the last years of the complex's existence. With an approximate area of 1.26 hectares, it comprised an administration building, four dormitory blocks, a kitchen unit, two toilet blocks, a laundry room and the tiny St Luke's church, all nestled in lush greenery. There was an infirmary intended for residents awaiting admission to hospitals or under observation for infectious diseases. A segregation block was for beggars and vagrants, suffering from addiction withdrawal symptoms or simply violent and self-destructive. The home's security measures were tight and followed the recommendations of the governmental prison department. This resulted in an entire apparatus of control, with barbed wire over the perimeter walls and metal gratings at drain openings—those who entered the home were often to leave it only after death. This is why the site is supposed to be massively haunted—a widespread belief considers mentally ill persons, especially the incurable ones, as obsessed with or possessed by ghosts, acting and behaving no differently from living ghosts, their souls remaining earth-bound after death. Places where such persons lived or passed through are therefore understood to be haunted by many spirits, even long after their demolition. Paradoxically, the area outside the homes was famously known for its spiritual *chi* (the positive spirit or energy of life according to Taoism), despite its inauspicious neighbors. Before everything disappeared, there were three makeshift altars along the quiet tree-lined road of Lorong Buangkok, leading up to the former Woody Lodge. They held several Chinese deities revered with offerings of oranges, strong *kopi* or *teh* (coffee, tea), and joss sticks. At one of the altars, a bottle with numbered dice

BUILT BY THE BRITISH IN THE 1920s, AND PRIOR TO BECOMING WOODY LODGE, THE COMPLEX WAS KNOWN AS TRAFALGAR HOSPITAL, A WELL-MAINTAINED ENSEMBLE OF SCATTERED PAVILIONS AND COVERED PATHWAYS DESIGNED IN TROPICAL COLONIAL STYLE (SOURCE: NATIONAL ARCHIVES OF SINGAPORE, CIRCA 1930)

indicated that superstitious taxi and lorry drivers went there to pray for their lucky numbers in the Singaporean pools. At night, one would see flickering candlelight, and occasionally hear the piercing screams of resident inmates—or ghosts—disturbing the quiet atmosphere. Kampong Lorong Buangkok is in the immediate vicinity of the lodge. In the city-state's supposedly last traditional *kampong* (village), residents enjoy a slower pace of life, with typical old-fashioned features: large wooden bungalows, verandas, orchards, and unfenced tiny gardens. But ghosts occasionally disturb them. Allegedly, villagers were possessed one night, and some became as mentally ill as the residents of the nearby homes. Coincidentally, the possession incident happened after patients had passed away at the lodge. The entire *kampong* population panicked and some residents moved away. The government plans for redeveloping the area are a more rational and immediate threat to the village's future than the ghosts. As for the lodge, all physical traces of the welfare homes have been erased and the *tabula rasa* operation is almost complete. The site underwent a complete rebranding, erasing any contextual awareness of its uneasy past. Advertised as "Singapore's public housing for the future," the new housing blocks will offer "vibrant places" and cutting-edge forms of "integrated living." It is ironic that government developers highlight "educational sculptures [in the park] from which children can learn exciting facts about local history" when in reality, any vestige of the place which once stood here has been expunged. But, because of the plethora of ghost stories around Singapore, it appears unlikely that the loaded past of an area linked to mental illness, solitude, and death can disappear altogether. The ghosts of Woody Lodge may wander around for a little longer, a reminder that no society is devoid of insanity.

11 Sep 86

BACKGROUND NOTES FOR PRESS DIALOGUE ON 26 SEP 86

WOODY LODGE

1 INTRODUCTION

On 14 Jun 86, the Bushey Park Home at Borneo Road for the reception, care and rehabilitation of destitute persons was relocated to its new premises at the former Trafalgar Unit of Woodbridge Hospital at Lorong Buangkok, Yio Chu Kang, Singapore 1954.

1.2 With the relocation, the Home was renamed Woody Lodge and was duly gazetted as a Welfare Home for the care and rehabilitation of destitute persons in accordance with the provision of the Destitute Persons Act (Chapter 98).

1.3 The Woody Lodge covers an approximate area of 12,649m^2. It comprises an Administration Block, Dormitory Blocks (4), Kitchen Block, Toilet Blocks (2), a Laundry Room and a Segregation Block.

1.4 The new Home was renovated prior to the takeover, Repairs and Redecoration Works (R & R) amounted to $115,000. This include repairs to roof, sunken floorings, ceilings, painting and replacement of windows. Minor improvement works as approved by the Development Planning Sub Committee (DPSC) cost $296,230. The amount included purchase of furniture and equipment.

2 SPECIAL FEATURES OF THE HOME

Several new features have been incorporated in the Home to meet the special needs of its residents. These are :

2.1 Sick Bay

There is a Sick Bay in the Home. It is meant for residents who have to be kept under observation, suffering from infectious disease, or who are very ill and pending admission to hospitals. The Sick Bay has a capacity for 4 residents. A slop sink is installed nearby.

2.2 Public Address System

A public address system was installed in the Home based on the recommendation of the Fire Safety Bureau. The speakers are located in the dormitories, dining hall and multi purpose hall. Besides important announcements, piped music are played through the PA system for the benefits of the residents.

"THE HOME WAS RENAMED WOODY LODGE AND WAS DULY GAZETTED AS A WELFARE HOME FOR THE CARE AND REHABILITATION OF DESTITUTE PERSONS IN ACCORDANCE WITH THE PROVISION OF THE DESTITUTE PERSONS ACT" READS THE "BACKGROUND NOTES FOR PRESS DIALOGUE" OF SEPTEMBER 26, 1986, WHEN THE TRAFALGAR UNIT OF WOODBRIDGE HOSPITAL WAS RENAMED (SOURCE: NATIONAL ARCHIVES OF SINGAPORE, 1986)

CLEARED SITE AT BUANGKOK
(SOURCE: SINGAPORE HARDWARE ZONE FORUM, 2016)

Dear Marcel

We refer to your email of 5 Jun 2015 regarding the former Woody Lodge building complex.

Last year, the site was cleared for the development of "Buangkok Square", which is a mixed use development comprising public housing and a neighbourhood centre. You may obtain more information of the development on HDB's website at the following link: www89.hdb.gov.sg/hdbvsf/eampu09p.nsf/0/14SEPBTOHGM_page_1112/$file/about2.htm#about2

For information on Woody Lodge, you may wish to refer to the National Archives of Singapore at www.nas.gov.sg/nas/ or other resources e.g. Google streetview which shows images of Woody Lodge.

We hope you find the above information helpful. Thank you.

Urban Redevelopment Authority § Physical Planning, North East Department § Privileged/Confidential information may be contained in this message. If you are not the intended recipient, you must not copy, distribute or use it for any purpose, nor disclose its contents to any other person. Please notify the sender immediately if you receive this in error § Check out our website at http://www.ura.gov.sg

EMAIL FROM THE URA TO THE AUTHORS
(SOURCE: URBAN REDEVELOPMENT AUTHORITY AND PHYSICAL PLANNING, 2015)

FROM 2003 TO 2016, THE RAPID AND MERCILESS SCRAPPING OF THE 1920s HOSPITAL TO BECOME ANOTHER PUBLIC HOUSING ESTATE IS BEST UNDERSTOOD BY SATELLITE IMAGES (SOURCE: GOOGLE EARTH, JANUARY 30, 2015)

SURYA HOME
舒雅疗养院

ATN. MALE STAFF
PLS. CHECK THE
NEW DUTY ROSTER
IN DINING HALL.
THANK YOU.

ALL STAFF
PLS. LOCK THE
GATE AT ALL TIME

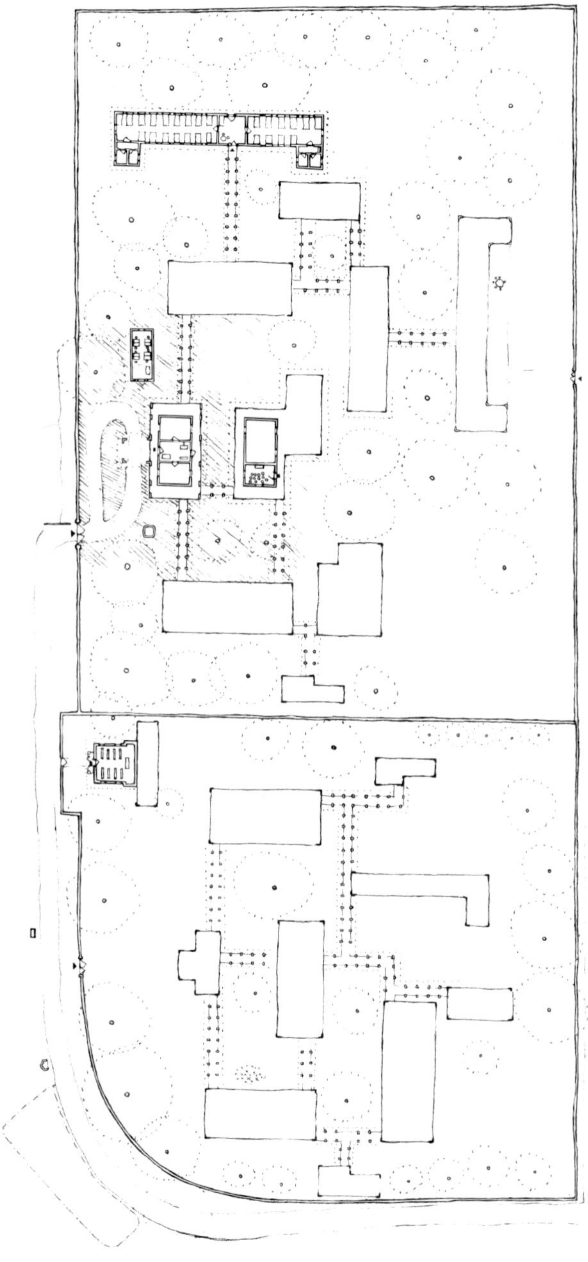

UNCOMPLETED DOCUMENTATION—BETWEEN CULTURAL HERITAGE PRESERVATION AND FUTURE ARCHAEOLOGICAL EXCAVATION

5

HAW PAR VILLA

1°17'03"N 103°46'57"E

262 PASIR PANJANG ROAD, SINGAPORE

BUILT IN 1937

ARCHITECT: HO KWONG YEW

COMMISSIONER: AW BOON HAW &
AW BOON PAR

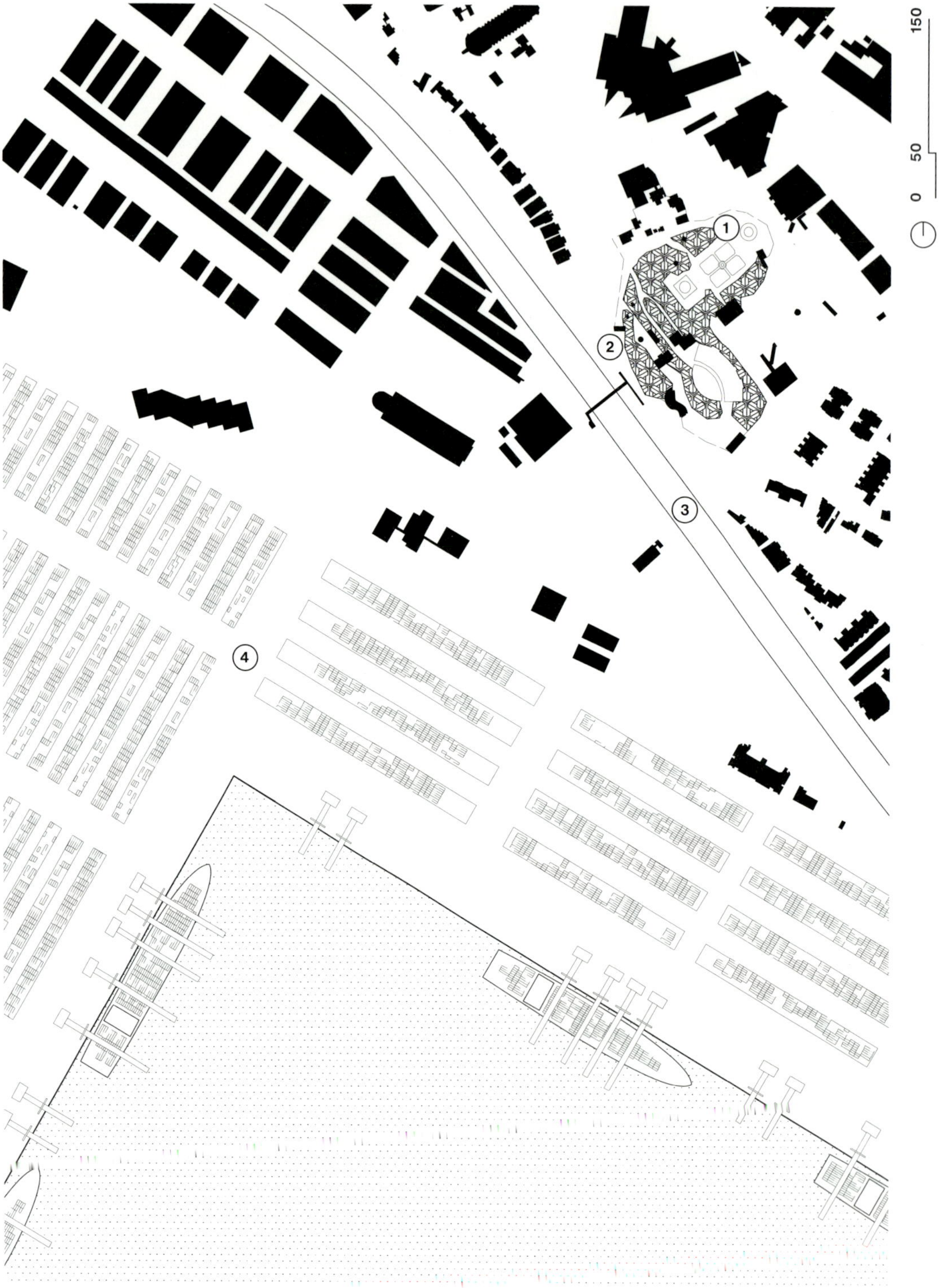

1 HAW PAR VILLA 2 GATE 3 WEST COAST HIGHWAY 4 PASIR PANJANG TERMINAL

If there is a place in Singapore that is officially haunted, it is this hugely popular, weird and dusty religious theme park. Named after the Boon brothers, the two Burmese immigrants who invented Tiger Balm, the villa was built by the older Boon Haw for his younger sibling Boon Par in 1937. Also known as "Tiger Balm Gardens," it is located on the slope side of the Pasir Panjang Road, in the southern district of Pasir Panjang ("Long Sand" in Malay), overlooking the harbor. At the time, the road followed the coastline, prior to the land reclamation developments of the 1980s and the construction of the container terminal in 1990. Along with the villa, a bizarre moral landscape was created, depicting Chinese folk traditions and mythologies, and what would happen if these were not respected and honored. Two other similar parks were built to popularize Tiger Balm products: one in Hong Kong, partially demolished in 2004, and one in Fujian Province in China, now a museum. The villa and the gardens were damaged during the Japanese occupation, but after World War II the thousands of demons, creatures, and ghouls that made the place famous were rebuilt. The most notorious section is particularly gruesome: the Ten Courts of Hell. Each court depicts, in graphic detail, the punishment awaiting those who commit sins. For instance, thieves and gamblers will be drowned in a pool of blood. A stone mallet will pound tax evaders, while moneylenders will be thrown onto a hill of knives. Cursing, misusing books, and viewing pornography will result in the sinner's body being sawn in two. Rapists will be flung into a wok of boiling oil. There is even a "Home Viewing Tower" where evildoers can see their family suffering as a result of their misbehavior. In the tenth court, the "Wheel of Reincarnation" will decide depending on the sinner's former life what he will be reborn as: human or animal, a good or a hard existence. The park went through financial ups and downs, and was taken over by the Singapore Tourism Board in 1979. In 1984, after various management firms failed to generate profit despite adding facilities (a dragon ride, a stage for theater shows, etc.), the park's entrance fees were waived, and entry is now free. School children are still taken there to learn good from bad, and post-visit nightmares are frequent. Everyone agrees the park is haunted. When it opened, the carcasses of stray cats and dogs were found at the entrance, and guards resigned after strange encounters during night watches. Some say the statues are really dead humans covered with wax, and offerings are laid in front of specific ones. Others say that a witch once sneaked in to connect with the other world, and summoned spirits who remain in the park, inhabiting the statues. Today, guards still hear screams and wails at night. Rumor has it that Haw Par Villa is actually one of the gates of hell. But rumor has it too that the Singapore Tourism Board is letting it slowly decay because of redevelopment plans for the 8.45-hectare area. The immediate

ALONG WITH THE "TIGER BALM GARDENS," THE BOON BROTHERS, THE OWNERS OF TIGER BALM, HAD A HOUSE BUILT ON THE PREMISES DESIGNED BY THE SAME ARCHITECT WHO DESIGNED SOONG SISTERS HOUSE. THE BUILDING WAS BOMBARDED BY THE JAPANESE FORCES AND DEMOLISHED IN 1940

THE POPULAR "TIGER BALM GARDENS" AND ITS ICONIC GATE QUICKLY BECAME THE STUFF OF YOUNG SINGAPOREANS' NIGHTMARES, 1960 (SOURCE: TIMESOFMYLIFE.WORDPRESS.COM)

neighborhood, the Pasir Panjang Terminal, will undergo major changes in the near future, with the container harbor to be relocated to another area of the island. Nine hundred hectares of waterfront land will be freed up for residential, leisure, and business purposes, directly opposite Haw Par Villa. Voices have already spoken up for the park, a sign of a certain attachment to the place. It is considered to be an exceptional example of Chinese superstitions, the last traces of a cultural heritage entirely wiped out in mainland China by the Cultural Revolution between 1966 and 1976. The last philanthropic garden in Singapore, it remains popular, perhaps because it may be haunted. It is almost as if the "physical" presence of spirits in the park was, in anticipation of change, preemptively protecting Singapore's most enduring ghost story. A sort of pedagogical, moralist playground, the now dilapidated brainchild of the Tiger Balm founder may be under the protection of its collection of concrete demons, sheltering this other world from evildoers, real estate developers and land speculators, who might think of its garish depictions of hell before coming too close.

LAND WAS RECLAIMED FOR THE PASIR PANJANG CONTAINER TERMINAL IN FRONT OF THE VILLA, DISCONNECTING THE AREA FROM THE SEASHORE. IN THE UPPER LEFT OF THE IMAGE, THE WHITE STRUCTURE OF THE THEATER STAGE INDICATES THE LOCATION OF THE PARK (SOURCE: MARITIME AND PORT AUTHORITY OF SINGAPORE, 2016)

PRIOR TO LAND RECLAMATION, HAW PAR VILLA WAS LOCATED ON THE WATERFRONT (SOURCE: PETER D. HUGGETT & COLIN PHILIPS, CIRCA 1980)

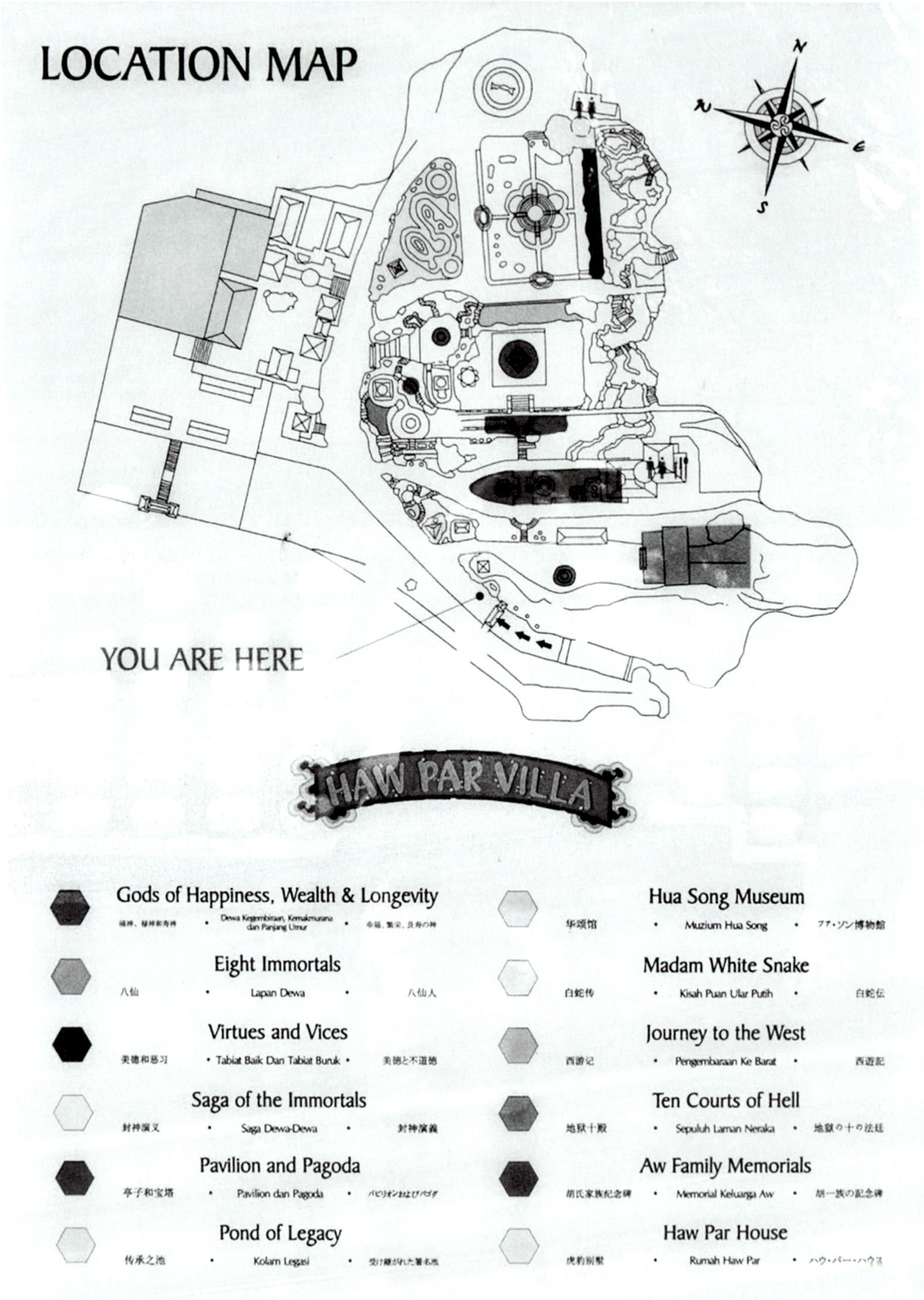

PLAN OF THE VILLA BY THEMES (SOURCE: CAVINTEAO.BLOGSPOT.COM, 2014)

S I N G A P O R E

HAW PAR VILLA - *One of the Park's main attractions is a slow boat ride through the gut of the dragon and experiencing the horrors of the courts of Hell.*

A RIDE INTO THE MOUTH OF THE DRAGON WAS ONCE A MAJOR ATTRACTION, ESPECIALLY FOR FAMILIES, IN WHAT WAS RENAMED "HAW PAR VILLA DRAGON WORLD," 1990 (SOURCE: CUPPALUX.BLOGSPOT.COM)

EXIT

PUNISHMENTS IMPOSED BY THE TEN COURTS OF HELL, AS SHOWN IN THE HAW PAR VILLA

虎豹別墅
HAW PAR VILLA

PAR VILLA

别

6

HILLVIEW MANSION

1°21'39"N 103°45'29"E

114 JALAN DERMAWAN, SINGAPORE

BUILT IN THE 1970s, DEMOLISHED IN 2007

COMMISSIONER: UNKNOWN

1 HILLVIEW MANSION 2 HILLVIEW ESTATE 3 BUKIT GOMBAK FOREST 4 BUKIT GOMBAK 5 MINISTRY OF DEFENCE

There is nothing left where the famous Hillview Mansion once stood. This mysterious "Green House," an unfinished private residence, was completely demolished after two landslides that buried all physical traces of the building. What remain are the iron main gates at the entrance to the property, a large plot of land at the end of Dermawan Street, close to Bukit Timah, central Singapore. The site has retained a certain popularity among thrill-seekers and urban explorers, attracted by fantastical ghost stories: a couple was struck and killed by lightning here, someone's mistress died falling from an unfinished terrace. Despite the site's complete spatial transformation, reports of wailings and sightings of mysterious globes of light continue. The story of this "unlucky" house gocs back half a century, when the Hillview neighborhood was first developed. Built around the Bukit Gombak hill, the estate was part of an industrial area, with factories scattered in the valley and granite quarries on the hilltop. By the 1960s these were all gone, and the factory lands were sold in order to erect private properties. In the 1970s, a car assembly plant was constructed nearby and its chairman started building Hillview Mansion for his mistress. Construction, allegedly stopped, never to resume, after the woman died on site. Official property records suggest that the land was only certified in 1980—it appears that the mansion was being illegally built. The property has changed hands several times since. Owned at first by Popular Estates, then acquired by Peaktop Property in 1987, three years later it became the property of a subsidiary of the Far East Organization, Singapore's largest private real estate developer. Located on top of a steep slope, next to residential houses and a condominium, with a splendid unobstructed panoramic view, the property could be considered a prime site. In the neighboring high-priced Bukit Timah area, close to good schools and the central business district, similar properties are sold for upwards of S$5 million. In the context of these dynamic real estate activities, the lack of action from the current owners of the phantom Hillview Mansion seems even more perplexing. Wild speculations twine around the two landslides that occurred in 2006 and 2007 too. After heavy tropical rain, the overgrown and unmaintained terrain below the house collapsed, damaging buildings at the foot of the hill. The mansion at this time was still partly intact. Oddly, the landslides occurred solely on the land surrounding the mansion, and it is suspected that these were used to justify the demolition of the house. Singapore's Ministry of Defense, one of the mansion's neighbors across the hill, covered the slope with tarpaulin, and soon after the land was leveled, terraced and sealed off with the help of cranes and other heavy machinery. It has since been turfed over and is heavily fenced off. Barbed wire and warning signs safeguard the entire hill, and the gates are padlocked. Stenciled characters reading *Private Property* are there to keep intruders at bay. Today, other than the scenic

HILLVIEW MANSION PRIOR TO ITS DEMOLISHING, 2002
(SOURCE: CHARLES GOH, ASIA PARANORMAL INVESTIGATORS)

gates, a large retaining wall painted a washed-out white and the outhouse for the mansions' electric generators are the only contextual remains of a site once ranked among Singapore's most haunted spaces. The site underwent dramatic change, from a dream home, to an unfinished, iconic haunted house located amidst wild tropical greenery, to a sealed-off, man-made, never-to-slide-again terraced slope. But despite these efforts, and even though the actual space that encapsulated the ghosts has disappeared, the ghost stories have not. One wonders to what extent the land's haunted status has kept it from being redeveloped. While it is true that interest in the obscurities of Hillview Mansion has declined, stories and legends about the place continue to circulate, testifying of the endurance of the supernatural in the human psyche.

THE SLOPE IS COVERED IN TARPAULIN WHILE THE REMODELING IS DONE, 2007 (SOURCE: IJAMESTANN. BLOGSPOT.COM)

WORKS ON THE TERRAIN. THE MINISTRY OF DEFENSE COVERED THE LAND WITH TARPAULIN AND COMPENSATED THE AFFECTED NEIGHBORS, 2007 (SOURCE: IJAMESTANN.BLOGSPOT.COM)

REMODELING OF THE SLOPE, 2007 (SOURCE: IJAMESTANN.BLOGSPOT.COM)

GHOSTHUNTERS IN FRONT OF THE MANSION'S REMAINING GATE (SOURCE: ASIA PARANORMAL INVESTIGATORS)

TOP: HILLVIEW MANSION AND ITS SURROUNDING SLOPPED TERRAIN IN 2003. BOTTOM: IN 2007, AFTER A LANDSLIDE THAT SPARED THE HOUSE, THE ENTIRE AREA WAS REMODELED AND THE BUILDING DEMOLISHED (SOURCE: GOOGLE EARTH)

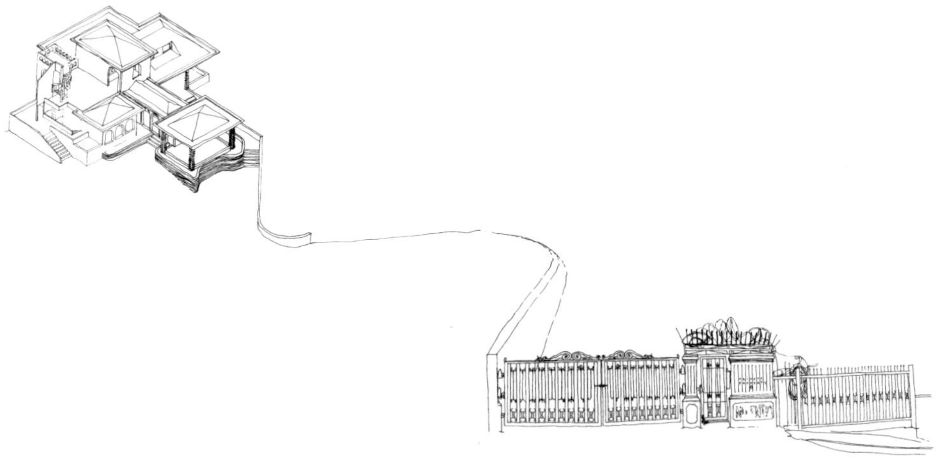

CONTEXTUAL REMAINS—THE MANSION IS LONG GONE YET THE RUMORS LINGER AT ITS GATE

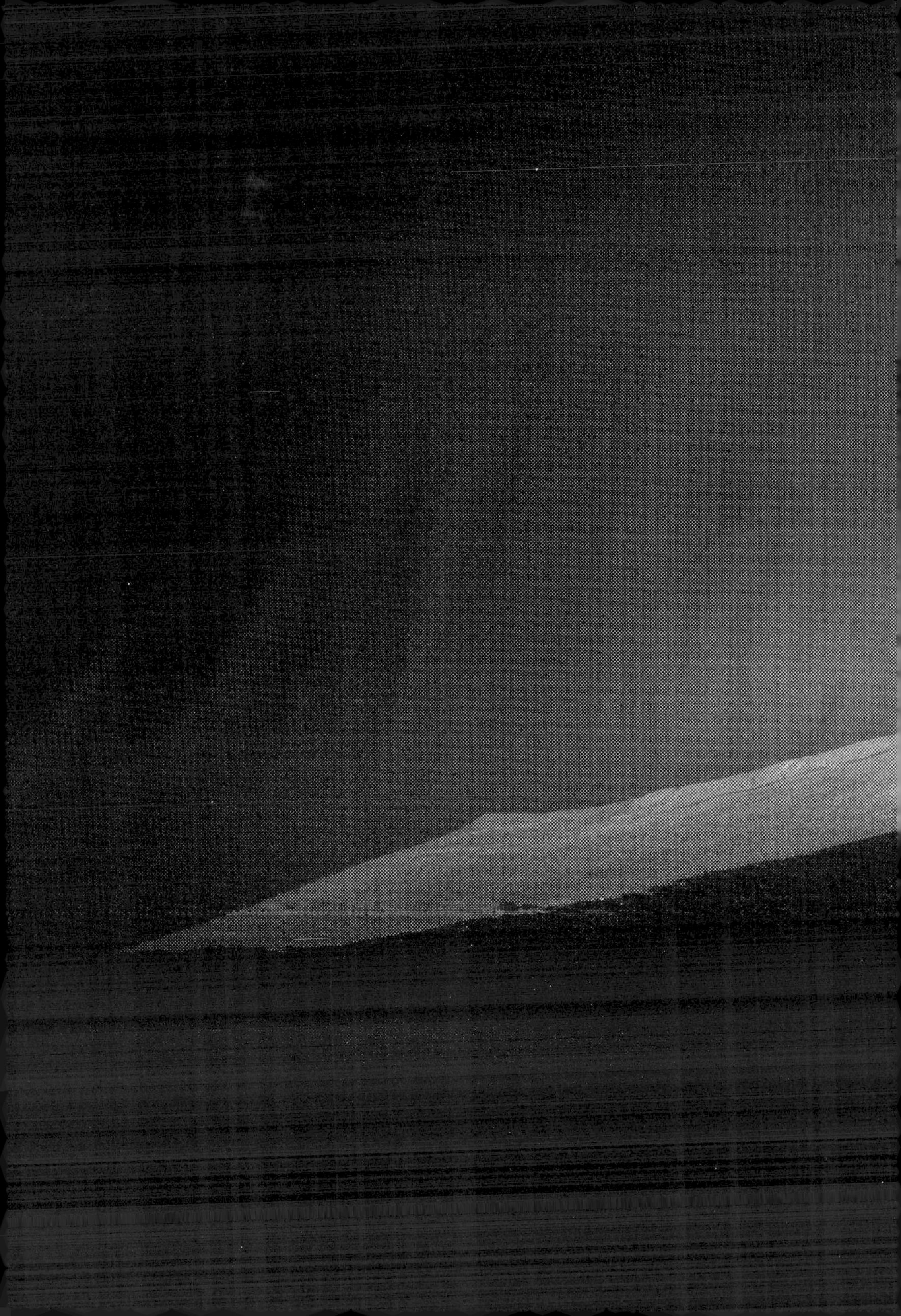

BISHAN MRT STATION

1°21'04"N 103°50'54"E

200 BISHAN ROAD, 17 BISHAN PLACE, SINGAPORE

CEMETERY IN USE UNTIL 1973, MRT STATION OPENED IN 1987

COMMISSIONER: LAND TRANSPORT AUTHORITY

1 BISHAN MRT STATION 2 CIRCLE LINE (UNDERGROUND) 3 NORTH SOUTH LINE 4 KALLANG RIVER 5 BISHAN PARK

Bishan MRT (Mass Rapid Transit) Station is a metro station serving the estate of social housing blocks of the same name in central Singapore. Nothing is left of the cemetery on which it once stood, yet locals say the whole area is haunted: the metro station, the trains, the park, the flats. Prior to the exhumations and cremations conducted by the authorities from 1979 to 1983, the Kwong Wai Siew Pek San Teng cemetery was the final resting place of Cantonese and Hakka Chinese immigrants from Guangdong. In operation from 1870 to 1973, it gave its name to the estate: Bishan is the phonetic transcription of the Mandarin *pek san teng*, meaning "jade hills." Once a sloped area with 50,000 graves and a few traditional *kampongs* (local villages) spread over 145 hectares, it was one of the largest on the island. The site saw fierce battles during World War II. Populations found shelter there throughout the Japanese occupation. Owned by Chinese communities, it became state property in 1978, after a six-year lease. At the time, the narrative of "land-starved

Singapore" made this development appear absolutely necessary and indisputable, and the clan members managing the graveyard did not object to its obliteration. In addition to having seen "phantom" train passengers without reflections and heard footsteps in the station corridors, locals claim that spirits chased out by urban development have taken revenge by triggering an "epidemic of suicides" in the neighborhood. Indeed, police reports mention a few cases at the nearby Bedok Reservoir. Initially, all this seems to have resulted in reluctance on the part of local people to move in when the estate was completed in 1984. Real estate prices at Bishan New Town remained low for a while, until the complete development of the area made it a popular district, complete with good schools and facilities. The adjacent Pek San Teng crematorium, whose 10,000-niche columbarium hosts some of the remains from the cemetery, is testament to the modern way in which death is dealt with today. There are claims that spirits have relocated there. If most inhabitants of Bishan say that they don't fear the ghosts, some admit to avoiding certain areas at night. It is indicative of a deeper sense of place that Bishan's past as a graveyard has not entirely disappeared from public memory, and is still vivid through ghost stories. Somehow, across the metro station, the housing blocks, and shopping mall buildings, the former status of the site shines through. While one might consider that the fate of Bishan is indicative of what to expect for the other large cemetery, Bukit Brown, or for any heritage site that stands in the way of development, times have changed. Singaporeans appear more aware of their heritage, and are ready to fight for it, and they might get ghostly help to do so.

ROOM FOR 30,000 MORE GRAVES

Free Press Staff Reporter

A COMMUNITY cemetery in Thomson Road in which stand the graves of more than 100,000 Singapore Cantonese and Khehs is to be extended because of congestion.

The burial ground, of 300 acres, is to have 100 acres added to it, which means room for an estimated 30,000 more graves.

An official of the Kwong Wai Sui community — which comprises most of Singapore's Cantonese and Khehs — said yesterday that an average of 100 dead were buried in the cemetery every month.

Burial at the cemetery is free although a small fee ranging from one dollar to four is charged for the digging expenses.

Work has started on the road leading to the new extension for the use of funeral processions and hearses. To expedite the work, the community association has been presented with a steam-roller by a benefactor, Mr. Fong Fook Tian.

The extension will be used for burial as soon as the approach road is completed.

Two temples, the community association's office premises, a school and a market are situated in the precincts of the cemetery land.

The Kwong Wai Siu runs a free hospital at Serangoon Road to attend to the poor patients of its community. It has 13 wards, one of which is a maternity ward. At the moment, there are more than 350 in-patients, of whom 160 are women.

IN 1950, THE KWONG WAI SIEW PEK SAN TENG CEMETERY WAS EXTENDED TO INCLUDE 30,000 MORE GRAVES (SOURCE: *THE STRAITS TIMES*, AUGUST 22, 1950)

Govt acquires site for housing scheme to link Toa Payoh, Ang Mo Kio estates

By

PAUL WEE

SINGAPORE'S biggest and one of its oldest Chinese burial grounds, the 113-year-old Kwong Wai Siew Peck San Teng cemetery, will soon make way for urbanisation like other cemetaries before it.

Tucked away deep in Kampung San Teng, off Thomson Road, the 146-hectare Cantonese cemetery has been acquired by the government for a housing project that will eventually almost link the Toa Payoh and Ang Mo Kio satellite towns.

No one knows exactly how many bodies are buried in the cemetary as a great part of its records was mislaid, lost or destroyed during the war.

Cremation

Still, the history of the cemetery, which has among other things, a century-old temple, a school, market and canteen, is the story of the Cantonese community's early pioneering work at starting a home for themselves in Singapore.

The government's acquisition is perhaps inevitable in land-starved Singapore.

Already, there are signs of development in the area. Over the past few weeks, workmen in convoys of lorries and tractors have been toiling near the fringe of the cemetery where an arterial road linking Braddell and Thomson roads is now nearing completion.

Although the days of the cemetery are numbered, the Kwong Wai Siew Peck San Teng federation feels that fullscale development on the site will not be immediate.

This is due to the large number of graves that need to be exhumed and their remains cremated. Also, the limited cremation facilities in Singapore will mean it will be a while yet before the job can be completed.

By any reckoning, this may take at least five years before the entire area is ready for development, according to the officials of the federation.

Its secretary, Mr Loh Poh Tuck, said its members endorsed the government acquisition on the cemetery, but they were unhappy because they had not been informed whether there was an alternative site for them.

He said: "We have no objections to the government's move to develop the area, but we are apprehensive because there has been no news whatsoever on the acquisition move.

"We require a place to relocate the ashes of our ancestors once the cemetery is taken away."

According to him, the cemetery was founded by the early Cantonese pioneers from the three prefectures — Kwong Fu, Wai Chow Fu and Siew Hing Fu — in Kwangtung province in China.

It was apparently initiated by a famous community leader then, named Mui Nam Swee — whose identity was borne out by a stone tablet carved in 1890 — who started a benevolent movement which led to the purchase of burial grounds in 1866.

In 1890, with improved means, the group constructed a temple and network of roads leading to the grave site. A memorial stone tablet in remembrance of the achievement was also erected at the site.

Two decades later, telephone service was introduced to the temple, and in 1957, a school was built to cater for the educational needs of the squatters living in the area.

The cemetery subsequently underwent reorganisation under which burial lots were properly marked out. It also introduced the "first-come-first-served" system to prevent misunderstandings among the superstitious clansmen.

The cemetery was divided into 10 sectors, built on the 10 hilly regions in the area. Each sector, which could accommodate 10,000 graves, also had a pavilion for visitors to the cemetery.

In the early days, each clan had its own sector, and only members were to be buried there.

"Time has changed all that and the practice was stopped after the war," said Mr Loh.

He added that besides the school, the federation had

Squatters

He said there were about 2,000 squatters living nearby and these people, who were mainly farmers, paid the federation a token monthly rent of between 50 cents and $5.

The Housing Board conducted a census in the area last year and Mr Loh hoped these dwellers would be resettled when the time came.

The federation yesterday conducted its annual general meeting at the Yeung Ching School in Chinatown, and it is understood that 16 chiefs from the various affiliated clans and the federation's executive committee were nominated to form a sub-committee to negotiate with the authorities regarding the acquisiton.

The sub-committee is expected to conduct a meeting soon to discuss the matter.

Meanwhile, as the remains of the members' forebears lie in peace amid the tranquillity of Kampung San Teng, there will be no rest for its living members who are preparing themselves for a busy time ahead — all for the "future" of the dead!

"GOVT ACQUIRES SITE FOR HOUSING SCHEME TO LINK TOA PAYOH, ANG MO KIO ESTATES." THE ARTICLE ANNOUNCES THE RELOCATION OF THE KWONG WAI SIEW PEK SAN TENG CEMETERY FOR WHAT WOULD BECOME THE BISHAN PUBLIC HOUSING ESTATE (SOURCE: *THE STRAITS TIMES*, APRIL 30, 1979)

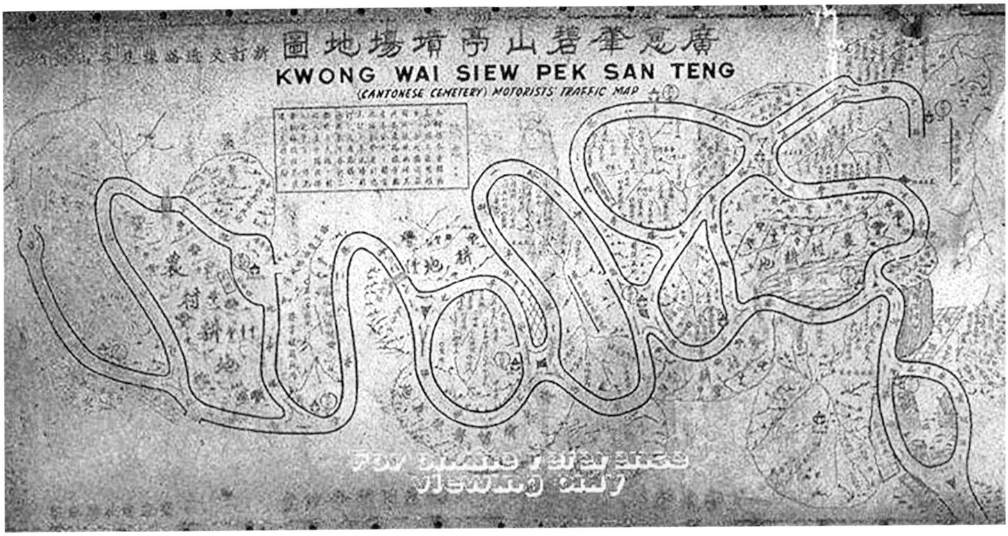

"MOTORISTS' TRAFFIC MAP" OF THE KWONG WAI SIEW PEK SAN TENG CEMETERY
(SOURCE: NATIONAL ARCHIVES OF SINGAPORE, 1978)

VIEW OVER THE GRAVES AT KWONG WAI SIEW PEK SAN TENG CEMETERY, 1960s
(SOURCE: MRTHANG.BLOGSPOT.COM)

NS17 CC15 Bishan

Circle Line
CC
NS17 Bishan
CC15 碧山
2 min
NS18 Braddell
布莱德
4 min
NS19 Toa Payoh
大巴窑
6 min
NS20 Novena

NS17 Bishan
碧山
OSIM
OSIM

LAYERED SITE—BISHAN NEW TOWN IS BUILT OVER THE KWONG WAI SIEW PEK SAN TENG CEMETERY, OF WHICH NOTHING SURVIVES, EXCEPT THE GHOST STORIES

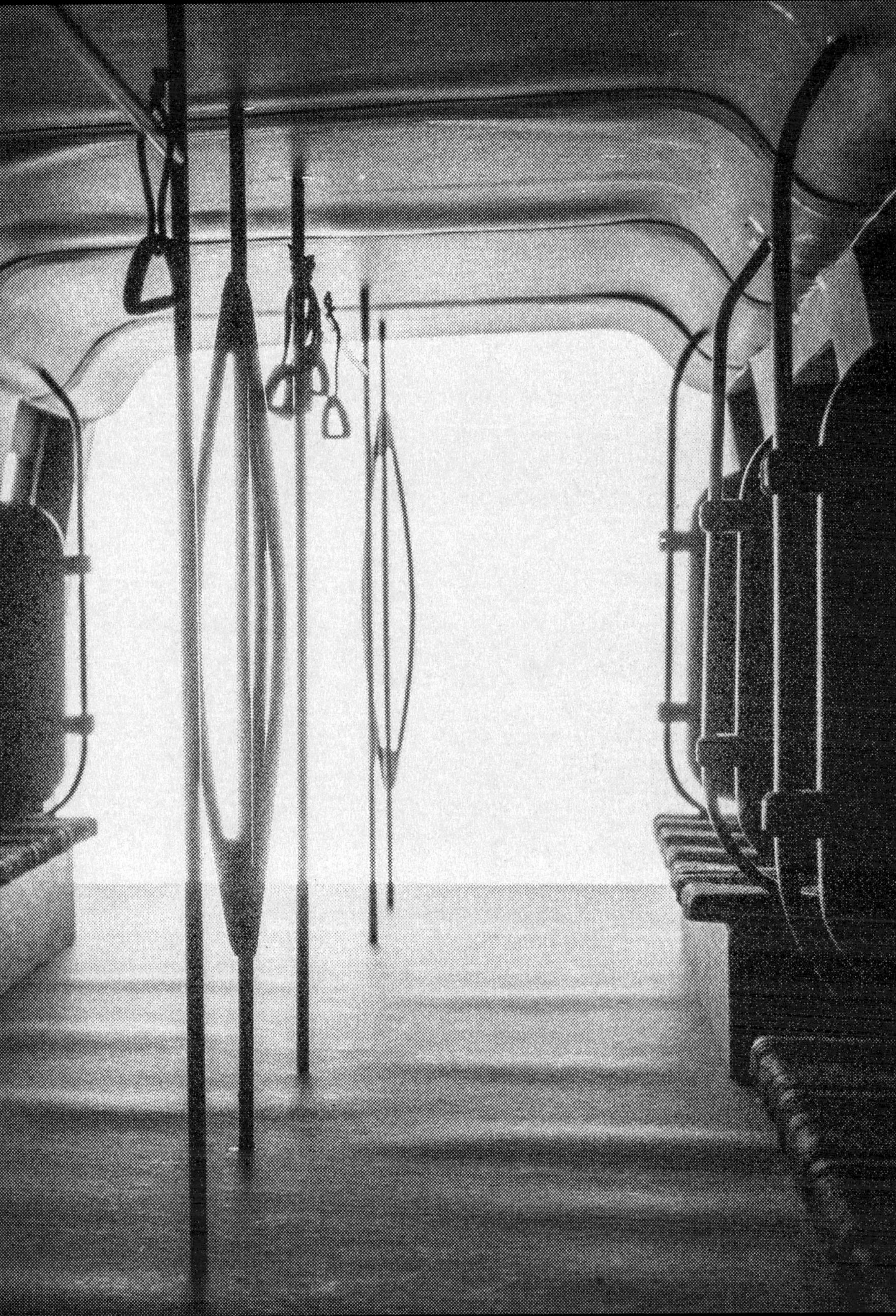

BUKIT BROWN CEMETERY

1°20'10" N 103°49'23" E

36C LORONG HALWA, SINGAPORE

IN USE FROM 1922 TO THE 1970s

PARTLY DEMOLISHED SINCE 2013

COMMISSIONER: ONG CHONG CHEW FAMILY

1 BUKIT BROWN CEMETERY 2 PAN ISLAND EXPRESSWAY 3 MACRITCHIE RESERVOIR 4 LORNIE ROAD
5 NEW LORNIE HIGHWAY 6 AREA AFFECTED BY EXPRESSWAY CONSTRUCTION

The taxi driver does not know the way, and struggles to find the rusty gates of Bukit Brown cemetery, located just south of MacRitchie Reservoir, in the very center of the island. The meeting point for this informal visit is under the old rain tree. Since 2005, passionate citizens—"Brownies," as they call themselves—have organized public walks that start here. The Goh brothers, well-known local ghost-hunters, claim to have sparked this interest by organizing nightly ghost-spotting tours. Looking for spirits among the beautiful, opulent graves of prominent entrepreneurs, politicians, Chinese pioneers—notable Peranakan matriarchs and patriarchs—and their forgotten ancestors, "Asia Paranormal Investigators" and a few others—for example, the Nature Society of Singapore (NSS) and the Singapore Heritage Society—have revealed a fascinating and fragile heritage in the lush jungle. Today's strolls will take visitors only to a few of the 85 hectares of the largest cemetery in Singapore, a fraction of the area covered by the 100,000 graves. Established in 1874, it was then known as Seh Ong cemetery, a burial ground for the Hokkien Ong Clan, located on an area called Kopi Sua ("Coffee Hill," due to the nearby coffee plantations). Its current name comes from the Malay word for "hill," *bukit*, and to the landowner of another plot, the shipping magnate George Brown, who sold it to the Chinese clan associations looking to expand the cemetery. The site started officially operating as a graveyard in 1922, at first only for Chinese Hokkien communities, growing steadily to include others on adjacent plots. Later on, the authorities acquired the land. This, the largest Chinese cemetery outside China, was closed in 1972, following governmental agendas promoting cremation while earmarking all cemeteries as potential land for development. Bukit Brown is obviously an important historical fragment of Singapore because so many of its pioneers are buried there, drifting in oblivion, but there is more to it than that. Large Art Deco graves and traditional Chinese horseshoe-shaped mounds, tombstones decorated with Japanese majolica or Dutch ceramic tiles, faded black-and-white enamel portraits of defunct fashionable ladies, and numerous statues of angels, dragons, and Sikh guards are only a few features of the incredible richness and variety in funerary architecture on display here. Bukit Brown also holds the topographic memory of the island. While hills elsewhere were leveled, the soil dumped in the sea for land reclamation projects (for example, East Coast Park), and rivers channeled into concrete ducts, its cemetery status preserved the area. It now offers an authentic image of the island before its development, a time capsule of a sort. The jungle, with its hills and creeks, is home to a rare fauna and flora, prompting the interest of botanists and bird-watchers. Yet, following the national narrative of land scarcity, official agencies—chiefly the Urban Redevelopment Authority (URA)—remain unimpressed by the

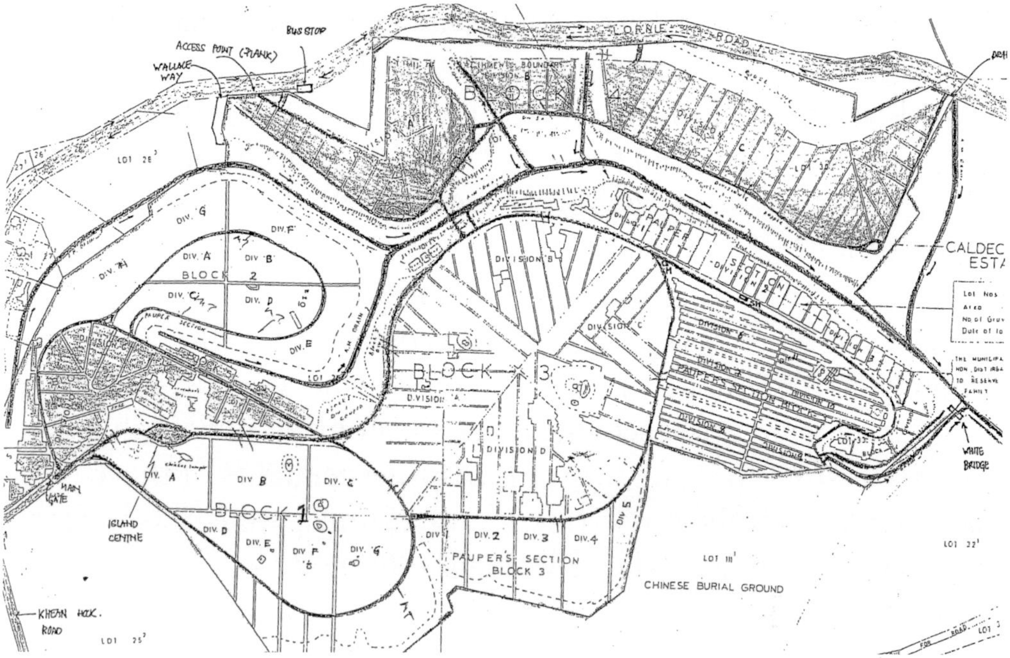

BUKIT BROWN CEMETERY IS ORGANIZED IN FOUR BLOCKS, THEMSELVES SUBDIVIDED INTO DIVISIONS AND SECTIONS, CONNECTED BY ROADS AND PATHS, SMALL RIVERS RUN THROUGH THE AREA (SOURCE: NATIONAL ARCHIVES OF SINGAPORE, 1973)

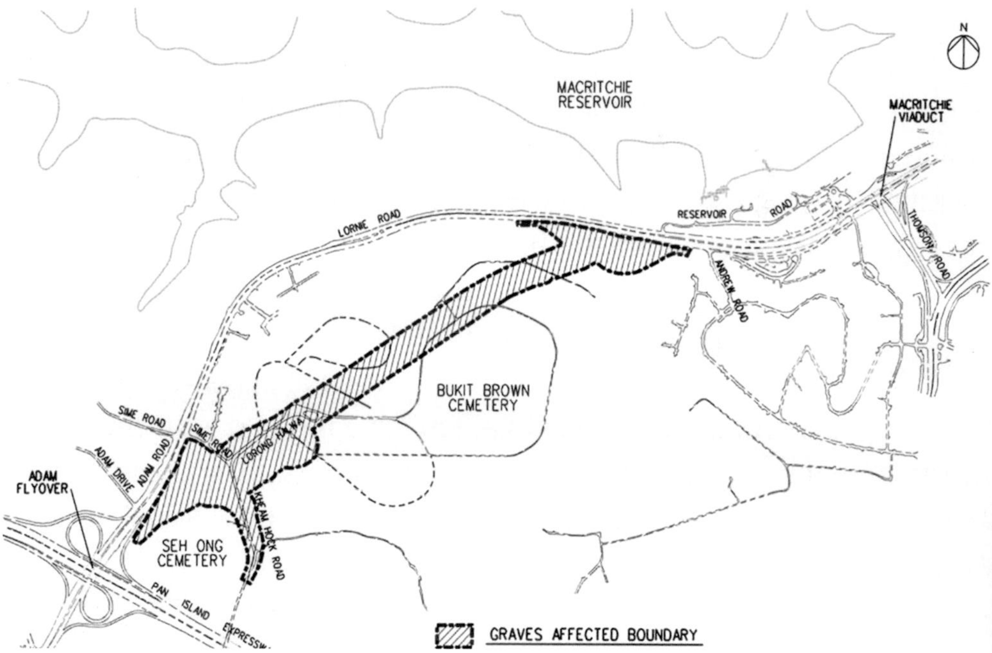

THE NEW ROAD SLASHES THROUGH THE CEMETERY, 3,500 GRAVES ARE BEING EXHUMED (SOURCE: LAND TRANSPORT AUTHORITY, 2012)

richness of this cultural landscape. Having stayed intact for so long, Bukit Brown is now under attack. An inoperative local transit station, Bukit Brown MRT, has already been constructed to the north of the burial grounds. While most of the area is untouched, a highway—the spearhead of a housing development planned for 2040 that will annihilate the entire cemetery—now slashes through the greenery, forcing the exhumation of 3,500 graves. In a society where opposition is discouraged, the project is highly contested and has prompted segments of civic society to organize in an unprecedented way. Forming an improbable union, ghost-hunters, history buffs, the descendants of those buried there, joggers, horse-riders, and wildlife enthusiasts were soon joined by journalists, genealogists, heritage specialists, intellectuals, students, and artists to defend Bukit Brown with online petitions, walks, blog posts, exhibitions, and press articles. Conservation groups such as SOS Bukit Brown and All Things Bukit Brown were founded. In 2014, the URA was challenged and the legality of the land-use master plan adding the highway was questioned, prompting a discussion in parliament. A motion was even filed—unsuccesfully—to list Bukit Brown as a UNESCO World Heritage site. It was nevertheless included in World Monuments Watch, a list of at-risk sites. The highway is now complete, but awareness has been raised. The URA has registered interest in the site and supports documentation of the tombs. More and more Singaporeans know about Bukit Brown, and what it holds. At such a rich site, where historical, spiritual, and natural values have merged, can the ghosts prevent the largest remaining cemetery in Singapore meeting the fate of other such landmarks, fallen prey to urban development?

DRAWING IN SUPPORT OF THE "SAVE BUKIT BROWN 100%" PETITION THAT SAW CIVIL SOCIETY OPPOSE THE ROAD, REFERENCING THE OCCUPY MOVEMENT, ANONYMOUS, AND THE ICONIC STATUE OF A SIKH GUARD FROM ONE OF THE CEMETERY'S GRAVES (SOURCE: SOS BUKIT BROWN, 2011)

SAVE OUR SINGAPORE
Our Nature Our Heritage Our Land
SAVE BUKIT BROWN

CATALOG OF MANY—THE COMPLEXITY AND RICHNESS OF THE CEMETERY EMERGES FROM THE MULTITUDE OF ELEMENTS THAT IT HOLDS, FROM MUNDANE EVERYDAY OBJECTS TO RITUAL SACRED ITEMS, THROUGH MAKESHIFT ALTARS AND FASTIDIOUSLY DECORATED TOMBS, TO EXQUISITE FLORA AND POLITICAL BANNERS

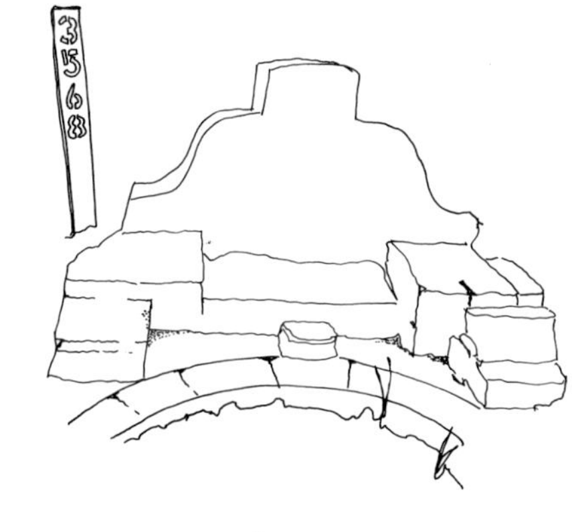
3568

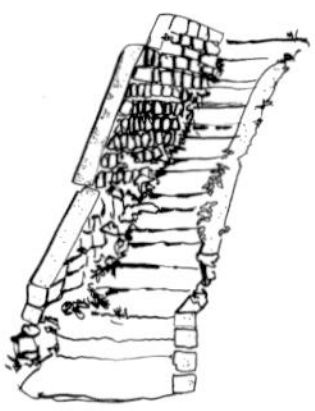

1876

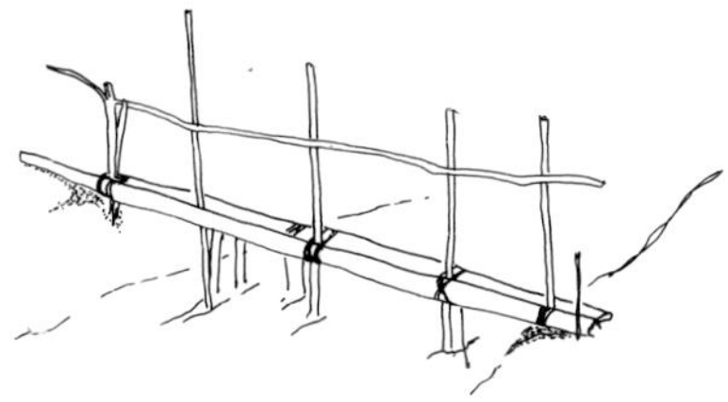

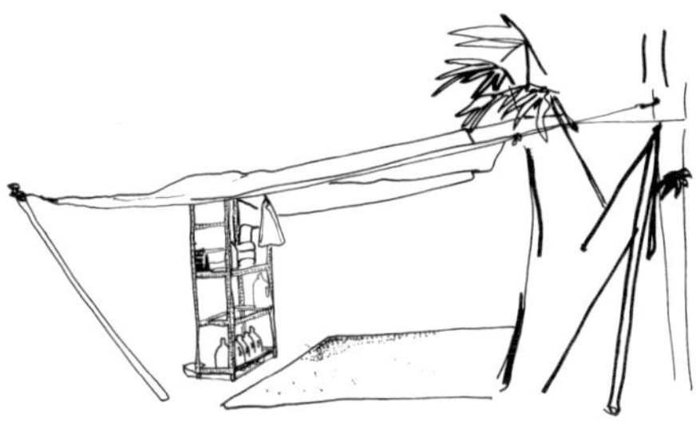

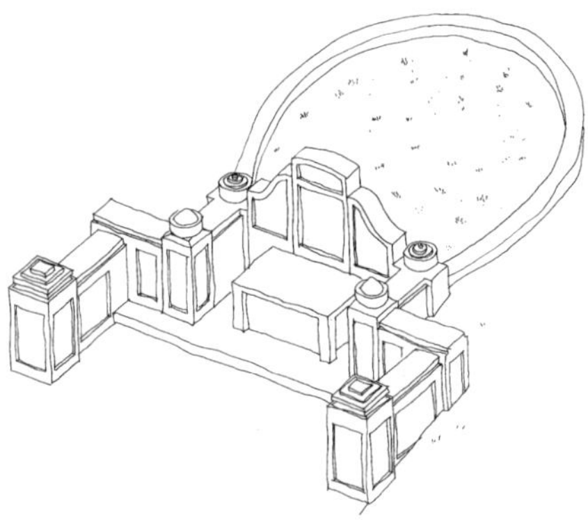

MADAME

INTERVIEWS
Denise L., Charles Goh, Jones Tang, Lilian Chee

INTERVIEW WITH DENISE L.
Bank employee, born and raised in Singapore
September 13, 2013
The Black Swan

CHARLOTTE MALTERRE-BARTHES We look at the moment when modern culture clashes with beliefs, and that's why we are investigating the spaces that are supposedly haunted. We are not interested in ghosts per se, but in why these places exist. They are typically abandoned places like Changi Hospital, but can be recent ones too. A friend claims her brand-new office in Bugis is haunted because in 2009 a guy went to the roof and jumped. Can you tell us more?

DENISE L. That's one part of it. A lot of haunted spaces deal with violent history. Bugis is a tragic story. The guy got really drunk after his wedding, and his wife was sleeping or in the shower, he went for a walk, and then he fell. He never committed suicide. Changi Hospital is famous for being haunted. The whole of Sentosa too, because of World War II. Japanese troops invaded Singapore, sending some of their battleships towards Sentosa. The army was kneeling in the water when they were killed. Now there have been stories about people drowning along Siloso beach, strong, confident swimmers, who would just drown. So, there are these stories about these areas being haunted.

CMB Saying a place is haunted is a way to make sure history doesn't go away. Because Sentosa looks like an amusement park now. It's a very good example of how popular culture and what people know about a place nevertheless leak through a perfect appearance.

DL Correct. And it is particularly interesting that over the past few years there have been Halloween parties at Fort Siloso, the most haunted place in the whole of Sentosa. It's almost like a museum there. It's opposite Labrador Park, and I looked across the sea and there was this creepy green-blue light around the whole area, and fire, and people screaming, because there was a ghost train going around. And it went on for two or three nights. So, there is some weight to this argument, but I'm not sure if I would phrase it like you have. There is some connection to the history of the place, but they always want to give some sheen to it and make it very modern. They want to make it interesting in a more pristine kind of way, than being really creepy and old, or as some place to avoid. Generally speaking, cemeteries are creepy, like Choa Chu Kang cemetery, a very old one, in the northwest, where the Christian and Indian graves are.

CMB But, for instance, Bukit Brown is not creepy at all. It's very nice, the graves are scattered, it's more like a park.

DL Bukit Brown is more historic. The most popular [haunted destination] is Changi General Hospital.

CMB We have been there. But it's being refurbished, so I think the ghosts moved out. Next to it is the Old SIA Group Sports Club that is abandoned and closed, and it's actually creepier than the hospital. One theory is that the ghosts moved there in the meantime. My colleague trespassed and went inside, but we never went there at night, as we are not interested in the ghosts, but in the space. Because if you go at night, fear takes over.

DL The current NUS Law and Public Policies Campus, situated on a hill next to the Botanical Gardens, is another example. I don't know the historical background, but I know the place because it was my university campus for a while. I personally find it very creepy, and I heard some stories about it. There is a student housing block built in the 1970s or 80s, very pretty, about, five or six storeys high. I heard it was pretty creepy. I just heard some stories: People studying there late at night or working on a project, they would hear slamming doors, but there would be no one around.

CMB Nothing visible?

DL Of course, you always have school ghost stories, like in a chemistry lab, where you open a door and there's a skeleton inside.

CMB Singaporeans are so into those kinds of stories. There is also a haunted HDB estate somewhere around Bedok Reservoir that has a famous haunted block, but they tore it down. Someone was murdered there in the early 1990s: a guy slaughtered his wife. The minutes of the court said that she was trying to kill him, so he killed her, explaining she was freaked out, or super drunk or drugged, but it was said in a way that sounded like she was possessed. And then someone came to help, and he also tried to murder that neighbor. He was hanged, of course. So that block was torn down. Bedok Reservoir, Block 16. Someone also told me that some MRT stations are haunted as well, perhaps because they are built over cemeteries.

DL Do you know the Bidadari estate, a new housing estate being built at Punggol, is on top of an old graveyard? It's going to be a new town soon [a public urban development including housing blocks and services]. There was some discussion about it on the internet: is it okay to build over this cemetery? Some argued that it has already been there for so long. Also, in the east, in the Siglap area, there is a place called Flamingo Valley, built over a graveyard. A few years ago, during the construction boom, some of my friends were looking for a place to invest in, they saw this condominium that was going to be built on top of the cemetery. When they heard that was over that particular cemetery, they decided not to touch it.

CMB That is an interesting mechanism related to real estate, a very tangible thing. If they hear ghost stories, Singaporeans can't decide if they should be very modern about them or scared. They would not buy a piece of real estate if they believed it was haunted. So in terms of economy, it has an impact. It's exactly that moment when history overcomes modernity.

DL I think we are very schizophrenic. But it is also because our parents, post-war baby boomers, were born into tradition but then over the past years they experienced modernity. So they passed on a lot of culture to us, and this is what we have grown up with. Maybe two generations on we will see the paradigm shift. But a lot of us are still very spiritual.

CMB I think this is partly related to the fact that Singapore developed so fast, and that there is nothing to cling to. And this relates to forms of spiritual resurgence.

DL I just got married. My partner's parents are very Chinese, and they actively remind us that there are traditions, our culture, and this is what we took vows about when we got married. This is what his parents told me. There is a tension between my husband and his mother, as she is a practicing Taoist. She insisted that his friends come to pick me up on our wedding day. So, these two friends had to sleep in the same house as him the night before the wedding, one even on the same matrimonial bed. I said no way. He had to tell his mother that his friends slept over, so she would calm down. His mother wanted to observe tradition. Tommy Koh, in *The Straits Times*, wrote this op-ed titled "Seven habits of a happy Singaporean." I thought it was a stupid headline, but quite an interesting write-up. He makes a point that Singaporeans cherish religion and racial tolerance. We can say things, and we can joke around, but by and large, I think we are very tolerant. And we frown on people who are outspoken against different religions. This is something that is very ingrained in our system, because our forefathers went through violent periods due to religious tensions. That is something that we have been taught in school, we are brainwashed, and we don't like to talk about it. You can believe in your own stuff, and we are not going to give a shit about it. But it works the same way in families as well.

CMB Saying that, don't you find disturbing that at places like Bukit Brown, where the pioneers are buried, it seems okay to plan to build over it? I find it very troubling.

DL We are a very particular society. It would be helpful to read what Lee Kuan Yew says. Yes, Lee Kuan Yew talks about very touchy things. On religion, he would say that he doesn't believe in a god, but he would never deny its existence. So he is on both sides, very practical.

CMB But he is also coming from communism.

DL That is the backbone of the system.

CMB But then how do you explain that everyone, regardless of their religion, believes in ghosts? Everybody, Chinese, Christian, Indian, everyone is freaked out if they hear a place is haunted.

DL I'm not sure if this has to do with religious tolerance or is more of a human condition—to believe there could be something else outside of this realm.

CMB My friend who told me about her haunted office in Bugis, she is very rational in many ways. But she believes in ghosts.

DL If you work there, and you feel something is wrong, you hear noises, or feel the sensation, you can't explain it through rationalizing.

CMB I asked my friend how she could tell it was haunted, and she replied, because things move. You leave your desk in the evening, in the morning it's completely changed. But there is no proof. We went to her office, and there were workers repainting, and I asked whether these were ghosts, and she replied: well, how do you know they are not?

DL [Laughs] It's interesting. I have friends who can see things, by this proverbial third eye, spiritual eye. When they were young, their parents were really religious; they were given certain Chinese Taoist blessings as a protection or offering to some kind of god. They got this blessing of the third eye, so they can see things. They can see things, or make comments on haunted places. This friend was in the Upper Serangoon area, she was at a house-warming, along with a couple of friends. She was at first very chatty, jovial, suddenly she became very quiet. Later she said: this place is dirty, meaning she saw some spirits. So even though you personally don't believe, you meet people who make you think twice. And then come the stories about a person who died here before, or committed suicide, or there was a murder, the place is dirty, there was someone doing some black magic here. It's like a conjuring of spirits. Also, there are female mediums, of two types: dirty and clean. The clean medium is the body for deities, or a voice. She brings a god to herself, or whatever idol, and then talks to it. The other one is the one that brings out the ghost. A friend whose mother is a clean medium, he has been exposed to many things like that.

CMB I think it is also a different entry point to understanding Singapore. As you know, there is this shiny brochure-like Singapore of modernity, the financial miracle. And here is this other entry point, a sort of dark, back-door entry.

DL Exactly.

CMB My partner in this project at the beginning was very rational, but since we have been visiting these places, he has been getting a little bit worried. He is dating a Singaporean girl and she doesn't understand at all why he is doing this. She is very serious about it and she thinks it's very disrespectful towards the ghosts.

DL Yes, if I would trip over, say, incense, I would instinctively say I'm sorry. It's something I have been told to do. It's a matter of respect, quite difficult to break the habit.

CMB I guess there is a culture of superstition.

DL It's also maybe both an Asian and a human nature thing, to be fascinated with this.

INTERVIEW WITH CHARLES GOH
Co-founder of Asia Paranormal Investigators and night-time safety manager on Singaporean construction sites
August 15, 2013
Funan Mall, North Bridge Road, Singapore

MARCEL JÄGGI How would you describe Singapore's relation to haunted places?

CHARLES GOH Singapore is rapidly changing and has a very short memory. The current generation has no idea about something that might have happened five or ten years ago—only the older generation may know. The memory of the young is non-existent. The youth are obsessed about finding jobs, earning money, making investments. If you compare ten years ago and now, there are fewer haunted places now than then. A lot of these places are disappearing, but paradoxically what is increasing is the belief. One in three of the younger Singaporeans would say they have seen ghosts, one in six say one of their friends has seen one.

CHARLOTTE MALTERRE-BARTHES I was just looking for Flamingo Valley, since a young Singaporean told me it was haunted and that one of her friends has seen ghosts there. I ended up on a real estate website where people were discussing the fact that they will not buy there because it's haunted.

CG The story of Flamingo Valley—I'm not familiar with it.

CMB It's just one of many we have heard.

CG A lot of the things on the internet are not based on any reality.

CMB That doesn't matter to us, because we are not really looking for the ghosts, we are looking for why such stories emerge. The story of Flamingo Valley proves the very tangible effects, the fact that some people said they have seen something and decided not to buy.

CG Oh, Flamingo Valley! It's next to a Muslim cemetery, a Bohemian cemetery, yes correct, it's one of the old cemeteries. So that place, they have been building it for a long time. So many years have passed and it's still under construction.

CMB What about Bishan MRT Station? It was built over a cemetery, right? When we were looking for the reasons why some places are haunted, we always found cemeteries.

CG Well, being above a cemetery is nothing unusual, because in the past our colonial government only controlled Christian burial, and not the other burial grounds. So, in the 1950s you can say that Singapore was like one big cemetery, but now Singapore is like one big construction site, so it's a kind of development change. Being above a former cemetery, there will always be stories, but only in the beginning: like Bishan when it was built, there were some ghosts underneath, old women and men. But this kind of thing fades away.

MJ What is your definition of a haunted place? What qualifies a place as haunted?

CG Before I answer your question, there are many people who want to do good, and those people look for abandoned places, because there's a belief that sad spirits wander there. So people would go there to sing songs and pray, but that does not really mean it is a haunted place, "haunted" means the place is abandoned, and because it's abandoned there is a cultural belief that there could be a gathering of spirits. So these places are haunted by a belief, or the fear of the unknown, and all these fears are exaggerated by what people are exposed to every day, like ghost movies, fear of the dark, the ghost movies that you see from Korea, Japan, Thailand. So "haunted" is not really associated with one reason, there are multiple reasons for such beliefs.

MJ So somehow, it's related to the age of a site or a building, for instance an old abandoned house. There are also new places considered to be haunted, but they are new so they aren't abandoned. You talked about the disappearance or the shrinking of the haunted places, and we are just curious about the new places coming up.

CG Life in Singapore is changing fast, it used to be forests here and there, lots of people died here. Lots of houses are abandoned; most of the land is owned by developers who are holding on to it because the land prices in Singapore are promising. They have no use for the land now, but the price will keep going up. For example, the cost of a piece of land in the 1960s, enough for a terraced family house, was 15,000 Singapore dollars, now it is 2.5 million Singapore dollars.

CMB You said haunted places are shrinking, but actually new places are haunted, like Bishan MRT Station. I have a friend who told me that her office in Bugis is also haunted, and it's a new building.

CG I have heard people claiming that their basement was haunted, especially if they live on the upper floors, but such stories are very far from reality. Because there is no historical background behind that, it's something we can't investigate. Singapore has a culture that believes, there is so much propaganda and we as paranormal investigators can't very easily believe everything. For example, just a few days ago, we received an email from a Brit or an American, who had just moved to Singapore. She said that she caught a few things, including objects moving in the room by themselves when there's no wind. She also heard kind of beeping sounds, she thought it was the cell phone; then the fan was being turned on by the remote. So, she says that the space is haunted.

CMB What about the big HDB estate which is known as haunted block, the government destroyed it, you know the one?

CG Of course the government doesn't destroy buildings because of ghosts. The government selectively demolishes buildings in the process of development. They decide that these buildings are too old, maybe because there are future plans for the area or the block, so they ask the people to move out, then they demolish at will. The government at the same time has kept many blocks empty within Singapore for emergency purposes, in case of SARS, H1N1, when they need to isolate the building or people.

MJ Do you know if the authorities look at ghosts as a kind of threat? Do you talk with people from the government?

CG I do have contacts, of course. Unfortunately, no, they are not concerned with that topic.

CMB In Bukit Brown, there's a mix between historical, haunted, natural values and a growing awareness of civil society. I think it's relevant to the general question of haunted spaces as form of resistance. That's most obvious in Bukit Brown, we don't know exactly how that translates to other haunted spaces.

CG I'm the pioneer who started all this in 2005 when I first looked into ghost stories—because I'm into ghosts—and I brought in my elder brother Raymond who is now the main defender of Bukit Brown. We discovered the cultural and historical aspects of the cemetery, but before that it was abandoned, it was a place known to be haunted, people went there for ghost-hunting. We have been cleaning tombs, conducting tours, and sometimes we ask for small donations, like gifts we give to the keepers for cleaning it. So the hauntedness in the face of heritage and cultural values fades. There are now more people who are concerned, and also people who say they saw something. Bukit Brown is unique because there are a lot of visitors, also the caretakers who maintain the cemetery have their own house. Three different communities used to live in a small village until 1970. Then of course when the government closed the cemetery, they left.

INTERVIEW WITH JONES TANG
Feng shui consultant and
ghost medium
February 15, 2017
National Design Centre, Middle Road/
office building in Bedok, Singapore

JONES TANG I work with haunted spaces, like many friends in Singapore who actually do haunted houses, and work with possession.

MARCEL JÄGGI What do you mean by "do"?

JT When people come to us because of trouble with the other world, we try to help as much as possible. We are able to do a lot of things, bring you to a lot of places and haunted houses in Thailand, Malaysia, Singapore. I believe many people deal with a lot of things related to the other world.

MJ We met a few of them, so-called paranormal investigators. They are offering non-commercial tours to haunted houses and are trying to shine a light on—you may want to correct me—that phenomenon.

JT What you are talking about—ghosts, haunted houses or even feng shui—I will give you a brief history of this. I might be wrong, and this is from my own knowledge. Our culture is very unique, because we have lot of races here, we have Chinese, Malays, Indians, Caucasians, Indonesians. So, we have a lot of gods in our world too. Chinese people tend to believe that when we die, our spirits will go to another world and will continue to live in that world. When the gates of hell are open, the "hungry ghosts" come to visit. It usually happens in August and September, because this is in the seventh month of the Chinese lunar calendar. The offerings you see in the streets are offered by us, the living.

MJ So how important is the Hungry Ghost Festival to the people?

JT In China not many people observe the seventh month. They separate themselves as northern and southern Chinese. Most of us Singaporeans belong to the southern Chinese. Northern China includes Shanghai, Beijing, and they don't really believe in the seventh month [the Cultural Revolution partially eradicated these traditions]. It's only the southern part—Guangzhou, Hong Kong, Taiwan, Singapore, Malaysia, Thailand—the southern part of China or where we emigrated. So in the seventh month, the gates of hell are open. The ghosts visit their relatives or even those who are not relatives, and they roam around the streets. It's like a holiday month to them, so we try to respect them as much as possible.

MJ It's a positive thing?

JT To a lot of the living, to us, it's not a positive thing, because there are all sorts of ghosts, from the good ones to the not-so-good ones, to the most hideous ones, to those that take a life just to replace their own. That is how we Chinese see things. If you commit suicide, as a ghost you will always commit suicide in the same area. Every other year, you will just jump down. So in order for you to break this cycle, you need to have someone to jump on your behalf. That is how ghosts are taking the living. That is why we have haunted houses too: many spirits have a great attachment to specific houses. They are always down here, in this world, looking for their houses. This happens until someone can see that cycle and help the spirits to be purified and get out of it. For that you need someone who is stronger than the spirits themselves.

MJ Who would that be?

JT Those are the priests, we call them "priests" in Taoism. The people who practice exorcism. It's purification only. To purify the spirits.

MJ Is there a kind of ceremony?

JT Either a ceremony or a negotiation between the priests and the spirits. As a child, I was not a believer but something was holding [possessing] me, until I was twenty-two or twenty-four when I asked for purification from a priest. He helped me so that I did not get harassed anymore. But the ghost was with me for about fifteen years.

MJ Sounds intense.

JT Spirits usually want to bring across a message that is not heard but felt. It's not a good or a bad message either, that depends on how you see things. That's why there is a negotiation between priests and spirits. In my case, the priest opened my eyes to things I was not able to see or feel before, and my senses are now there with the spirits. At that time of the purification I had extremely high sensitivity for a lot of things around me. With friends, as kids or teenagers, we always visited haunted houses. We didn't go there to get scared. We would ask what we should be looking out for, what we should not be touching and so on. I will not say anything more. I still have a bit of this kind of sensitivity. But it's gradually going down, because I asked for closure.

MJ You must be very knowledgeable about some "specific communication" with spirits?

JT It's more about personal experience. Because I never do the negotiation part with them. I never talk, or rather I never go into a kind of deep conversation with them. They know I can see them, but I never go into engagement stuff with them.

MJ So why you think this is mostly happening here, in this part of our world?

JT I'm not sure. The whole thing is made of two major parts. One you would call the superstitious part which is related to religion and a lot of things, one is related to science. I study mostly the science part—probably because my senses were opened by the spirits during my younger days. So, I have a very strong interest in the science of it. I believe everything in this world is based on energy, whatever we do is always energy. You cannot possibly go to the cemetery and be happy about it, you cannot stay down there and say you are happy about it. If you are extremely sensitive to guests, to this kind of universal phenomenon, or even energy, you get easily affected by it. That is the science part. Now we go back to religion. How does one get involved with possession by spirits or ghosts? This is a part of the creation that the Chinese have been trying to solve. We believe in another world, different to ours, a promise. Asians always believe that there is this other part, and that we have to obey the rules of that spirit world. That is how we keep ourselves in check as a good person.

MJ You are talking about people being possessed by deities, gods or ghosts. It doesn't suddenly come to you, I suppose. Is there a specific setting for spiritual possession or does one need to be purposefully open mentally, to prepare psychologically?

JT The psychological part plays a part too, but is linked to culture. Here, most people who actually get possessed by deities [spirits] or a god are Chinese or Asian. That means that they are imbued by their culture, that of their parents, and their belief in ghosts and gods. As a Caucasian you might not get possessed unless you are strongly rooted here from an early age, and you are immersed and familiar with our culture. This is how you might get affected. As an example, my Christian friend was possessed by a deity [spirit] that did horrible things to him. Christians, because of the religious difference, usually don't get possessed, but my friend is ethnically Chinese and psychologically he gets affected anyway.

MJ Talking about culture and the fast changes that are affecting or shaping culture, would you say this phenomenon is fading away nowadays? Are people less affected now compared to back then?

JT Maybe. I will not say entirely because there are always people trying to keep their culture intact to prevent it from fading away, and to pass it on.

MJ We met Singaporeans who said they don't believe in ghosts, but who still do offerings and rituals, just in case.

JT This is cultural. People do these festivities with their families. So, whether they believe or not, they choose to do it as a precaution. To me, that's one step into belief. A friend of mine did not believe in ghosts, but then a god appointed him to do stuff for him. Culturally, you are always imbued with it, unless you are Caucasian, or you believe outside this culture altogether. But as a Chinese, wherever you go, you will always be part of Chinese culture.

MJ You were saying that you have a certain sensitivity towards situations, towards the other world, towards ghosts. Do you also have that towards ghosts that are not part of the Chinese world?

JT I see things, a lot of things. I saw things from the age of eleven to twenty-four. Be it Chinese, Malay, Caucasian, even Japanese, I see it. I even went to Europe, to London, and I saw it there too. The local ghosts I mean. When I see spirits, there is no such thing as god or religion, there is no difference because of one's culture. For the past ten years I have not seen anything regarding gods, or other divinities. You are talking about possession, haunted houses, mischievous ghosts, I've seen them all. If I tell you we are not the only ones sitting in this café right now [the café is empty], would you believe me?

MJ I believe you. But not because I also see them here, but because I believe that other people can see them.

JT That happened to me a couple of times, while we were having platoon talks during my National Service days. There were forty of us in a room, but it was actually 150 of us including the ghosts. I see them everywhere. All I have to do is keep quiet. They are hanging around us listening to what we are doing. It can be scary, but usually it is normal to me.

MJ May I ask what you actually do?

JT [Laughs] Feng shui is my passion, my interest, I studied to professional level. You see a lot of people giving feng shui advice and counseling, but they are mostly unprofessional and are doing it out of commercial interest. Not me. I use word of mouth, and I do it for friends. Partially because it is my passion, and secondly when I studied, I studied for my own interest. Then when my friends started to ask what might help them, I started to look for them, how to look for things using my years of study. Then I used a lot of statistics, and it's continued throughout the years.

MJ Do you work with architects and planners when they come up with the new design and planning proposals?

JT No, I don't work with them! Because architects don't listen! Singapore architects don't listen, only a few of them listen. As a feng shui consultant you need to have common knowledge, common sense too, you can't just agree with what architects want to do, so that's why there are some conflicts. I only work with architects from Malaysia, on a project-by-project basis. But then the owner needs to find me. I go with them to the site, and I'm very particular. If I go to the site, and if I find the site no good, I tell them not to waste money on me.

MJ But that's after they have already bought the plot?

JT That's why I'm very particular, people say I'm difficult to deal with. Because if I find the site is no good, no matter how you build, it's no good.

MJ How do you qualify "good"?

JT The direction, the size of the plot, and what the surrounding of the plot is like, plus I need to touch the soil. It's just like selecting beans for coffee, it's the same for the plot.

MJ I have a question that is only indirectly related to the ghosts. In Singapore, twenty-five per cent of the land is reclaimed—new land, with an uncertain history, a history beyond recognition. Land is taken from rivers in Cambodia or some islands in the Indonesian archipelago. Ultimately, that is altogether a sort of artificial endeavor, and the history part is completely lacking. This land is reclaimed in order to build on it. What is your view on this?

JT It's still land. I'm talking about the type of soil. If they are using clay, for instance white clay, it's not good for humans, you create a lot of bad energies with that. When you bury a corpse, you want to bury it in good soil because you want it to decay properly. You don't bury in clay, because the body won't decay. This also brings bad energy to all your generations down the bloodline. We believe this creates a lot of health problems for you and succeeding generations. So, selecting sites for buildings, first I ask to dig the soil, six feet down.

MJ When does your consultancy start?

JT It's always better before they buy the place. I say I will go with you free of charge, just asking for transportation costs to be covered. The rest I cover myself. But if you buy the site, be prepared: I might walk over it, and tell you what I think. I don't want you to waste your time and money, or you mine. I'm not just any commercial guy, I don't do this to earn my living. Because if something happens to you later, it's my problem. I don't want to be the one to cause you health problems—because I know there will be a health problem.
For instance, bad soil always takes energy. Direction is another problem. If I know the place has, within a five-kilometer radius, a power plant station, or even power cable running through it, then it will be a problem. If you just go there and build, I will wish you good luck and go away. To all of my clients I tell the truth! Because it is in my interest.
It is true that in recent years my charges have become a bit higher. If people are willing to pay, I'm willing to help. But people think, if I give you the money, you do it for me, but it's not the way to do it. Some think money can buy everything—buy crystal to attract bad energy, but the whole bloody thing doesn't work like that. That's why my clients always come back to me, not because of feng shui, because of the truth.

MJ Your clients must have a plot, or they will sell a plot, they are somehow part of the real estate business. The question is: how do ghosts, or notions of hauntedness, affect real estate prices? Will that push down the price, because people are not willing to buy or are less likely to buy?

JT If the haunted house has been there for past centuries, and then suddenly urbanization arrives, it's not that everybody just wants a flat there. You can see it not being sold or built over for twenty years, because these stories are going around. For the stories to be completely gone, it takes one generation.

MJ This is what happened to Bishan.

JT The story of Bishan is still floating around. It's just that it's getting less and less, because fewer people get to experience this. It's Bishan and Braddell Road [a former World War II battle site], these two are the most prominent sites where the people have experiences.
I have a cousin who experienced something in Braddell before, someone tapping on her shoulder. She turned around, but she didn't see anybody. But that story was about twenty years ago. Eventually it will die down, and it will go to what the market needs.

MJ You could use those stories of ghosts as a real estate agent and make up a story, you could use the notion of hauntedness in order to push the prices down. Is there any manipulation taking placc involving ghosts?

JT You mean that property agents might use ghost stories to push the property price down so that they themselves can come in and buy at a lower price, am I right? I'm not sure about other countries, whether they do that, to allow them to get a lower price, but in Singapore and Malaysia, the market is too small. Talking about cities like Kuala Lumpur or Malacca, you need to have back-up stories for this to happen, that means you need to follow the stories from newspaper cuttings, Google and so on.

MJ We came across a ghost map of Tokyo, where a group of people marked every haunted house they were aware of. Consequently the surrounding houses and their real estate value were affected. Unsurprisingly, people in the market were very outspoken against this map, and they asked it to be taken down because it was not good for their business.

JT Actually, we have seen people here doing that too. It was a generation ago. But to prove that a place is really haunted, there are two simple steps: bring a kid, under three years old. Bring him to the house. If that kid will step in, play around in the house, jump around in the rooms and not stop for anything else, then the house is clean. Because kids have an extremely high sensitivity for energies. If the kid stops playing or starts talking to imaginary friends? Then beware. That's step one. The other step: bring a dog, a very young pup. A black dog. Black, because in our culture, black dogs have a high sensitivity for the paranormal. They are usually used to cleanse unnatural stuff too, whole houses if necessary. These two are enough [to prove hauntedness]. Why not cats, you might ask? Cats are too independent. They will not listen to you. A dog's mentality is the same as a kid's.

MJ What if the kid is not showing any kind of reaction and the dog is?

JT If the kid's or dog's reaction is not aligned, you can bring both in. If the kid is just very quiet, in one corner—usually kids will not do that, if they come to a new place. It will take some time for them to warm up. The moment they warm up to the place, they start to play around the whole house. They are quite active. If they start to quiet down, something is wrong with the house. Then you can carry the kid around in the house and just ask the kid: "How do you feel?" Ask simple questions. They will tell you if they don't like the house. They will give you all sorts of reasons to get out of the house. Or they cry. Very simple. Dogs will just bark. And they will always bark in one corner, looking at one place. These are the two simple steps. I always use a Chinese compass. Our compass is actually a vacuum. The needle will start to flop up and down. Because of the vacuum the needle will float up and down and will detect positive and negative energy. If it goes up, meaning positive energy, the good ones are there. If floating down, negative energy is there. If it doesn't move it's neutral. Every time you move from room to room, the direction of the compass should not be diverged more than fifteen degrees. That means the structure is either built on a certain magnetic field or the structure itself has a history of being haunted.

MJ Did it ever happen to you that someone has a house, with ten rooms for instance, but only one is haunted? Do you still transform and refurbish the whole house then?

JT No, it will still be there. Because the spectrum of the house is the whole spectrum. It means that the energy of this one room is the energy of the whole spectrum. It's always there unless you dig it up, the soil. You don't refurbish the house, you rebuild it, redevelop it. It means there is something wrong with the land itself. The room itself you can just seal off, like a storeroom, a non-existing room, but it is still there. Of course, you must look at how big the property is. If the property is very big, then you use this room as a storeroom. I experienced that in the army camp, in our barracks: one room was sealed to be a storeroom. That is in Changi. The same is in my company. I was also never able to step in that room. The moment I step in, I see things. It is not very nice. But we have also recreation rooms, one is transformed into an operation room, a planning room. I also suggested not to sit inside, as people could get sick, not because the air-con is blasting on high, but because of the spirits there. Initially they didn't follow my advice, but people would get sick, so there is evidence.

MJ Your clients are businessmen, property owners, companies, and private individuals, but how about the planning authorities?

JT I try not to get involved too much with the authorities, because they see us as superstitious, especially in Malaysia. If the authority has already approved the urban planning, I can tell property owners exactly which part of their plots they can use as industrial areas, for housing and so on.

MJ So you help to assign different kinds of functions to specific locations?

JT We can go far as about a ten-kilometer radius, but not over that. I can always tell you where to stay for your own sake. Feng shui usually kicks in in the earlier stages of the development, but whatever happens twenty years down the road, we cannot be sure, because there will be a lot of changes. So urban planning is definitely not my business. In feng shui we have a saying that every twenty-years the energy of the whole system changes, which means in the next twenty years, we can't do anything about it. Don't get me wrong, I'm talking about twenty year cycles, not duration. This means that you are still able to get different energy within these cycles, also positive energy. Because buildings usually come with a lot of other things: economics, population, and the place itself.

MJ But you will still be able to make some predictions?

JT We can do it, because the calculations for the next twenty years are already out, it's only based on numbers, and the numbers are out. There is a formula. But we also must take into consideration the economics, the population of the place, what attracts people to stay in that place. In feng shui we work in order to harvest energy. To get to the fast-flowing energy, you can open your doors a bit, and the windows towards the river, to allow this energy flow. We always associate buildings with elements, in Chinese culture there are five of them: fire, water, wood, metal, earth. They complement each other, but they are also against each other. And we always associate buildings with this. At Orchard Road for instance, everything is built in that way. If you see how the buildings are built, it follows this rule. In Suntec City you have the fountain of water in the center, in order to harness energy from everybody who comes to the property itself, to make you spend.

MJ If you look at the entire Singapore, it really developed in the last decades, all the new towns.

JT Yes, but even new towns are built according to this rule! Because it's embedded in the culture, whether you believe it or not. It goes for haunted houses too; we are part of that culture. If we are being told there are no ghosts, that we live in a place with no ghosts, truly there are no ghosts. In Chinese culture we value strongly family values, and that our ancestors are also ghosts. Our world is not based on God; it's based on ancestors. That is why our family culture is very strong. So, our religion is only meant for us to find peace, but if we don't have peace at home, then we start finding peace outside. That's how we see religion. Our whole culture has nothing to do with religion, it's only doing Confucian thinking, and Confucius is only about family. This is what people misunderstood, thinking that our culture comes from spirits. It's about respecting your family, your teacher, do what your teacher says. The problem is that along the way, people are exposed to a lot of other things. We want change, and this is what we will teach to our kids too. Respect your parents, granddads, and then you will get the respect back. That is our culture. So how did haunted houses become haunted? It's due to the fact that we believe in them.

INTERVIEW WITH LILIAN CHEE
Associate professor, Department of Architecture, School of Design and Environment, National University of Singapore
July 16, 2018

CHARLOTTE MALTERRE-BARTHES As a Singaporean academic trained in architecture, how do you reflect on the fact that spiritual beliefs are so strongly rooted in the national psyche, and how do you see the corresponding spaces playing off these beliefs?

LILIAN CHEE The animistic world is strongly rooted in Southeast Asia, with small roadside shrines set up spontaneously by groups of people around old trees, and particularly in suburban spaces where there is the possibility of overgrown nature or a secondary jungle adjacent to organized development. In Singapore, this sentiment is further bolstered by the Chinese "folk" religious belief systems which have syncretically adapted to urbanization and rapid redevelopment. Although organized religions such as Christianity, Hinduism and Islam have strong followings here, folk spirituality and animistic beliefs are practiced widely as they become part of everyday existence, even in domestic circumstances, and as such, are most affected by changing spatial configurations. The Chinese religion mirrors or augments the spatiotemporal life-courses of individuals. Religion is taken not just as a spiritual source for contemplation and discipleship, but more significantly, it becomes a pillar for managing one's worldly existence. People pray to deities and give offerings in exchange for passing school examinations, getting jobs, securing a good life partner and children, sustaining good health, attracting wealth, and enjoying longevity. The Chinese folk system is further manifested in a series of spaces outside of what one would consider as religious buildings or in the case of the "purist" Chinese religions (Buddhism and Taoism), temples. In the 1960s, these subsidiary spaces included clan houses, secret society associations, and funeral houses. In July every year, we see various ways in which prayers and offerings for the Hungry Ghost Festival (celebrated in the seventh month) are manifested in public housing estates, private residences, and among business establishments. Small open spaces, shared corridors and stairwells, void decks, roadside carparks and pavements are temporarily colonized by makeshift "altars" furnished with offertory wine and food. The air is choked by ashes suspended in the ether in the aftermath of the burning of "hell paper" in shared metal canisters which become the community incense burners. In these simple practices is the evidence of the rationalized city (the organized communal incense burners) and the ephemeral belief system (cakes, wine and fruits laid out in the open, to be devoured). In this, we see the enigma of urbanized existential religiosity—on the one hand governed by the city's rules and on the other hand, sustaining intangible folk beliefs. Each prayer offering is individual, and yet there is an unspoken understanding of how residual spaces can be mobilized by taking turns. The aftermath of the month-long religious practice is that the city, normally spared from litter, is dotted here and there with debris. Municipal workers are hesitant to dispose of these offerings for fear of attracting the wrath of the said deities. The offerings deteriorate in the hot and humid weather. They become a feast for rats and birds. These transform the clean city. The event has an aura of organicity in more ways than one—moving between unseen spiritual forces and the feral needs of animals surviving in a harsh urban environment.

CMB You are researching the cemetery of Bukit Brown, which became a space of contestation as well as of expression of national identity. What first interested you in that space? Could you see other cases/spaces that have a similar potential to cause a similar awareness, and if so, why?

LC My interest in Bukit Brown, a 140-year-old Chinese cemetery, comes from its complex constitution and entanglements. It has been treated as a historical and heritage site, but for me it is so much more complicated than that, and in its complexity lies the richness of this cemetery. My own entry into the cemetery began in June 2015, at a time when Bukit Brown was already in the middle of things: a confused entanglement of cemetery–jungle–heritage site–anthropological dig site–construction plot–media subject. A cemetery to be bisected by a highway, and then slowly naturalizing and forgetting itself until hallowed ground turns to neutral land: this marks the early stages of a tabula rasa in the making. Yet at Bukit Brown, the difficulty is compounded because this landscape is still actively remade and reimagined every day, crisscrossed by multiple routes, practices, and witnesses, urgently bearing upon the urban planners' abstraction of empty land. The cemetery refuses to play dead. Indeed, Bukit Brown has never been more alive than it is today. This tension gives it the very possibility of being both a space of contestation and an expression of national identity. Both qualities are not mutually exclusive. In this cemetery they coalesce. Long neglected since it closed for burials in 1973, the cemetery is notorious for many things, not least its inaccessibility. Families and individuals visiting ancestral tombs during the annual Chinese Qingming [tomb sweeping] Festival, which usually takes place in April each year, were known to trek through thick tropical undergrowth, risk bites from mosquitoes, ants, leeches and snakes, and struggle in search of tombs consumed by the ferocious growth of the jungle. Completely overwhelmed by tropical flora and fauna, and nestled in unexpected wilderness within the overall schema of a concrete island, a visit to Bukit Brown offered something of a primal return to a place lost in time, a kind of unmanaged organicity very far removed from the extreme orderliness of the over-manicured city. Its aura—encouraged by the landscape's heady mixture of obscurity, neglect, and subsequent wildness which altogether fueled the correct prospects for lurking spirits—also made this cemetery conducive to what lay at the fringes of society: disreputable activities such as faction fights, robberies, murders and black marketeering, and illegal swopping of burial plots when it was still open for burials, and more respectable animistic and temple rituals in the present day. Yet, I would argue against the overtly cultural interpretation of this cemetery, since this would overwhelm and dismiss that which is at the fringe of culture—the animistic forms, the spiritual practices, the rituals which happen each year. In fact, why Bukit Brown lingers in the imagination, and what its presence construes, is something that needs to be discussed. Yet, the cemetery has been catalogued primarily as an "object whose presence needs to be explained" rather than "a presence whose object-like appearance needs to be thought about." To rethink the "presence" of Bukit Brown beyond its status as an "object" of culture or of nature is to find ways to articulate this space wherein the conventional boundaries between culture and nature, the spiritual and the secular, absence and presence are ultimately broken down. This is why Bukit Brown fascinates me so—I want to understand and find a way to talk about its enigma.

CMB When we explore the relationship between spiritual beliefs and space, one evident connection is that of multiple layers of use, multiple successive practices, and perhaps through that, the creation of an identity—the tragic element comes on top of that. We see a sort of mechanism of resistance in believing in the "hauntedness" of a place, in perpetuating the stories around a building that is at times long gone. Can you see that too?

LC The aura surrounding purportedly haunted spaces has a strong affective pull. Affect is a pre-personal, pre-emotional intensity or feeling. It is sensed bodily rather than rationally. It is largely intuitive, and it is rooted to the way space organizes itself around us. There is no haunted house without the apparatus of the house and its accompanying structure of family and the family tragedy. Haunted spaces in Singapore are similarly those which have a long and ambiguous history. This past is often marked by an incident shrouded in death, trauma, or accident. No one can say for sure what happened, but the space stands as a witness to this unknowability. This is the affective sense of space which the award-winning Singaporean filmmaker and director Tan Pin Pin captures in her short film *The Impossibility of Knowing* (2010). We are shown an abandoned house, a canal, a green field and two apartments among other spaces, and we sense that the camera is "looking for something 'other' that might designate these as sites of previous trauma." On the green field, we see joss paper and sticks scattered at a grassy patch. This was where a tunneling contractor was buried alive—his remains were never recovered. We can call this a spectral landscape. The spectral implies a kind of unsettling; the ghostly or a haunting; of something that can be conjured; of something which somehow returns, or what Jacques Derrida calls "revenant." The cemetery's "haunting" effect, its otherworldliness, is an excess inimical to the concepts and vocabulary given to talking about empty pieces of land in Singapore; narratives which ultimately limit any description to enumerating and making visible all that is there while at the same time eliminating that which is uncertain or unknown as trivia at best, or non-sense at worst. In this sense, the hauntedness of a space has critical weight. It shifts not just the way we feel, but how we look, what we see, and what we value. Following Derrida, the spectral is rooted in place and yet connected to a constellation of spaces and times; it is defined by contemporary spatial practices and yet shaped by what is more-than-human. Most of all, the spectral suggests a different kind of seeing, and a need for an imagination which does not trivialize that which we cannot see.

CMB Finally, we also see some patterns in the spaces that are believed to be haunted, mostly related to death, which is universally understandable, but at times also simply because of events more remote historically, or even just because they are old. This appears to be something more "Singaporean." Can you see a connection between this pattern and the high-speed development of the island? We have underlined this as "the paradox between modern planning and spiritual beliefs." Can you see how this paradox is articulated? How is the "spiritual" embedded in the (allegedly) "smart" city that is Singapore? What is the role of the planning authorities in this and how did/does it evolve?

LC This question is in a way connected to my previous answer. Singapore is a conundrum because it is both modern and ancient at the same time. Its belief systems are rooted in the spectral landscapes which pop up every now and then, and subsequently disappear. The ancient belief systems see space as a plenum—a space that is completely filled with matter both physical and spiritual, or indeed that one is a consequence of the other. As such, even if space is erased and redeveloped, this plenum still exists, with the new development now acting as another layer to what was there. In this sense, the folk religions are deeply spatial and materialist in their manifestations and conceptions. In this already filled space, every action bears upon the space, as the space reciprocally exerts something unseen upon every action. As such, there are always negotiations, whether formal or informal, to mediate between these transient folk-religious practices and the insatiable capitalist urge to raze and rebuild. Spiritual mediums are brought to bless a plot of land, offerings are made and celestial "permissions" are sought before the first pile is dropped into the ground. This is not unlike the Ancient Greek practice of digging the *mundus* before building the city. The popular geomantic art of feng shui, for example, frequently intersects with architectural plans. The principles of feng shui are intrinsically spatially enacted. The geographer Brenda Yeoh emphasizes that it "unifies the geological, atmospheric, aesthetic and psychological qualities of the environment in one theory and code of practice." In this way, it is much more intuitive and prescient than codes of planning and design, which are separated and often oppose each other.

HEARSAY FROM A HAUNTED ISLAND
The Paradox between Modern Urban Planning and Spiritual Beliefs in Singapore

Marcel Jäggi, Charlotte Malterre-Barthes

> "Singapore's development should not and need not come at the expense of our heritage, our identity and our sense of belonging [...] But we do also need to make hard choices on how our land is used. That is the reality that we face."
> — Minister of State Tan Chuan Jin, 2012

Having a drink in the evening with a Singaporean friend in the Bugis district of downtown Singapore, we made our way to her office nearby to pick up something she had forgotten. Before stepping into the pristine lobby and just as she pulled out her entry pass, she cautioned: "Be careful, it's haunted." It was all there in that simple sentence: the unexpected, even improbable paradox of a fast-growing technocratic island populated by people with an enduring belief in spirits. A transcultural and transgenerational legend has it that ghosts pervade spaces all over the city-state, a collective conviction that to this day remains deeply entrenched in everyday life.

A DISCIPLINED NATION

An economic sensation of Asia, Singapore has tactfully curated its skyline, its business district, and its mass-housing program, not to mention its signature image as a peaceful, sleek, techno-modern metropolis. The country is technically and socially engineered, its constricted territory having been assertively developed after gaining full independence from Malaysa in 1965. Since then, the nation has been thoroughly urbanized and has economically outperformed all its Southeast Asian neighbors. With its 720 square kilometers and population of 5.6 million, Singapore is the world's third-densest country after Macau and Monaco, while being one of the wealthiest as well, boasting the third-highest GDP per capita worldwide and exorbitantly high real estate prices.[1] Natural resources are scrupulously managed here: water flows are meticulously channeled in faultless concrete ducts, dwindling green spaces are confined to functional use alone, parks are carefully manicured and monitored, and any unbuilt-on spaces have already been designated for future urban projects, where new condominiums or Housing & Development Board (HDB) projects planned by eager authorities will soon rise to keep pace with the city-state's already fast-paced cycles of urban renewal. Still, the rational, hyper-Cartesian logic that has reshaped the nation is shot through with ghosts and spirits, the specters which, it is said, are encountered everywhere on the island. So while it might at first appear quite unusual to advance an esoteric reading of Singapore in view of its alleged spiritual presences, the fabled haunting takes on an undeniable physicality in the spaces of this island nation, even if no ghosts are ever really sighted.

The disciplining of Singapore's population has been pursued through uncompromising territorial planning and social engineering (i.e., ethnicity distribution in HDB projects, electoral maps) carried out under the benevolent dictatorship of the People's Action Party (PAP) that, with its capitalist predilection for cost-effective success stories, has adopted a top-down approach to governing the city-state. In 1959, the British government—just prior to being ousted—had commissioned the first comprehensive master plan for the entire island that foresaw the extension of the historical urban city core and relocation of remaining agricultural faculties to the north and west of the island. But the master plan would never be implemented. The British had failed to defend the island against the Japanese Imperial Army in 1942 and, after regaining power, their grip withered in the years following the war. In the general election of May 1959, the People's Action Party won a landslide victory. Singapore became an autonomous state within the Commonwealth and declared total independence from the United Kingdom on August 31, 1963, only to briefly join the Malaysian Federation before leaving in 1965. Lee Kuan Yew, the young PAP secretary-general, would rule uninterruptedly as prime minister until 1990, when he finally stepped down, first succeeded by Goh Chok Tong, and later by his eldest son Lee Hsien Loong. Under Lee Kuan Yew, the government recognized early on the inherent limits of the 1959 British master plan, especially its classical central core and periphery approach, skeptical that such a strategy could cope with the rapid transformation that the country was undergoing. The congested, slum-ridden city-state faced a multitude of challenging urban development issues at the time: a shortage of housing with adequate sanitation and hygiene facilities, rudimentary transportation infrastructure, and a substantial portion of society dependent on backyard farming for sustenance. With the support of the United Nations, a team was appointed to reformulate a long-term framework for urban development. Its recommendations eventually led to the launch of the State and City Planning (SCP) project in 1967. Land-use planning had to address the two top priorities of a newly independent Singapore: the provision of adequate housing and the creation of employment opportunities for the people. The result was Singapore's first spatial concept plan, which served as a blueprint for the country's physical development for the next twenty years. The Ring City Plan bears a strong resemblance to the Randstad in Holland, constituting a total urban socio-spatial infrastructure. It authorized the development of a ring composed of new high-density satellite towns around the central water catchment

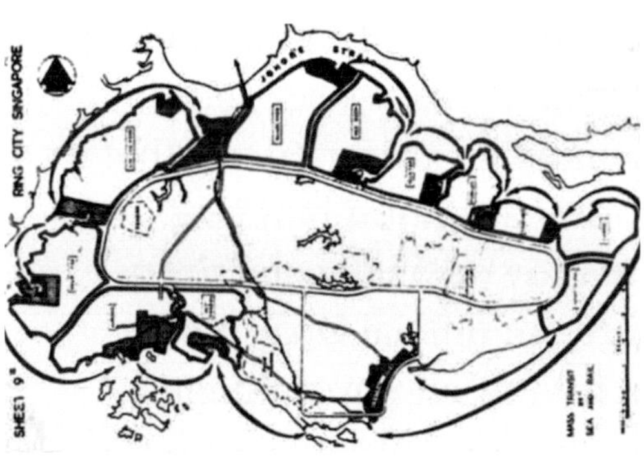

1963 RING CITY PLAN BY UNDP TEAM LED BY OTTO KOENIGSBERGER (SOURCE: SGARCHPERSPECTIVES.BLOGSPOT.COM, FEBRUARY 1, 2012)

area of the MacRitchie Reservoir, with each town separated by green spaces and a system of parks; the plan also specified provisions for industrial estates as well as a network of public transport linking all facilities. Its ambition and scope notwithstanding, the scheme neglected to take into consideration existing land use on the island, endorsing instead the superimposition of a technocratic urban vision of progress and development as if upon a blank slate.

The Ring City Plan was revised and updated in 1991 to steer the development of four regional centers outside the historical core to further reduce congestion. It was again revised in 2001 and 2003 with a superseding concept plan that aimed to make Singapore a "thriving world-class city." This strategy succeeded in transforming a nascent, newly independent nation into a mature, sophisticated, and sovereign country. The fast-tracked pace of implementation and change remains a distinguishing feature of the nation's particular planning drive. Scholar Brian G. Field has pointed out that "planning in Singapore is essentially a top-down process, with the political hierarchy setting goals which the state bureaucracy then translates into policies and programs for subsequent implementation. In this way, social and economic change has been carefully shaped to ensure political stability and continuing national prosperity."[2] While this is undoubtedly the case—or at least the ambition—in many other places around the world, it is the sheer speed and rigor with which the planning mandate is carried out that sets Singapore apart from other efforts at nation-building. One indispensable tool of the agenda to systematize territory is the Housing & Development Board, an official government institution that stands as the "armed wing" of government policies. Essentially a massive public housing program, it has been key to expediting the Ring City Plan. The HDB was developed in the 1960s in accordance with the model of "new towns," and by 1985 some 530,000 standardized housing units had been built. Supported by the government, the HDB was granted landownership privileges in order to implement its 100-per-cent home-owner program. Lee Kuan Yew explained in 1985 how this was achieved: "When we were confronted with an enormous problem of bad housing, no development, overcrowding, we decided that unless drastic measures were taken to break the law, break the rules, we would never solve it. We, therefore, took overriding powers to acquire land at low cost, which was in breach of one of the fundamentals of British constitutional law—the sanctity of property. [...] So we acquired [land] at sub-economic rates."[3] The large-scale, monotonous and anonymous architecture produced by and for the HDB are still today typically high-rise, high-density buildings between fifteen and forty-five storeys high, the spread of which has resulted in a homogenized residential landscape. Conceptualized and produced at industrial scale and built with prefabricated materials, the HDB model was considered a fast and efficient means for overcoming the housing crisis following independence. Traditional villages (*kampongs*) were razed to make way for the modernist housing blocks in which people were resettled collectively. The procedure for obtaining a HDB flat follows a relatively straightforward process and today more than 80-percent of Singaporeans live in one of the estates. The HDB is a state-owned statuary board and funds Singaporean citizens, who can benefit from a public loan to access temporal property based on a ninety-nine-year leasehold, guaranteed by their personal pension fund (Central Provident Fund—CPF). Citizens are indebted to the state to keep their apartment and are thus compelled to be continuously employed. It comes as no surprise then that Singapore's unemployment rates are comparatively low. The flat allocation system takes account of tenants' ethnicities to avoid an unwanted concentration of Malay and

Indian minorities, with state officials claiming social tranquility as the primary objective in their orchestration of a certain class mix. This said, the calculated social distribution by district also serves to produce electoral maps favorable to the ruling party by preventing a sufficient voting mass from electing opponents to PAP members of parliament (MPs) who are traditionally supported by the ethnic Chinese majority (74-percent of the population). This inherent means of social control has been acknowledged: "The public housing program did coincide with a genuine need for substandard housing to be replaced, but the need was met in such a way as to neutralize opposition and induce political loyalty [...] and reflected the primary political goals it acquired: the supremacy and legitimacy of the Lee faction."[4] Lastly, only traditional family types (i.e., the normative heterosexual household) and single persons over thirty-five years of age are eligible for HDB flats, thereby excluding non-traditional families from acquiring new units on the public market.[5] Since 1978, the HDB has also introduced incentive schemes to encourage parents and their married children to reside as neighbors. Promoting the continuity of extended family schemes as desirable, if not essential to national well-being, the government discourages any form of welfare or

FROM VILLAGE TO FLATS: AERIAL VIEW OF TOA PAYOH NEW TOWN. TOA PAYOH WAS THE FIRST NEW TOWN BUILT AFTER INDEPENDENCE, 1967 (SOURCE: MINISTRY OF CULTURE COLLECTION, COURTESY OF NATIONAL ARCHIVES OF SINGAPORE)

state-provided care for the elderly, reducing any such benefits to an absolute minimum. All such measures point to a deliberate and systematic social engineering that is intrinsically underwritten by urban planning.

REMODELING TERRITORY: "DO YOU WANT ME TO LOOK AFTER YOUR DEAD GRANDPARENTS OR DO YOU WANT ME TO LOOK AFTER YOUR GRANDCHILDREN?"

The disciplining of populations in Singapore has a tangible territorial correlate. Over the last thirty years, the island has reclaimed 140 square kilometers of land from the sea, amounting to a 25-per-cent net increase in state territory made possible by draining swamps and wetlands as well as strategically dumping soil in the ocean. At first, additional topsoil was sourced from leveled topography taken from the hills in the domestic central area, and later with volumes of sand acquired from Malaysia, the vast Indonesian archipelago, and most recently with Cambodian and Burmese sand, which has stirred geopolitical tensions in the region. Most of the reclaimed land has been explicitly designated for military and industrial use as well as for transportation infrastructure, and all such areas remain highly restricted. Recent studies have shown that public access to the shoreline of Singapore has been drastically reduced to a mere 7-per-cent, in effect turning the sea into a remote, visual backdrop of urban life that is off-limits to most, thereby prompting a fundamental reassessment of what it means to live on an island.[6] The profound socio-spatial impact of the island's ongoing spatial transformations, having dramatically alienated people from traditional cultural spaces, has been the subject of academic and arts scrutiny.[7] The destructive impact on vegetation is even more blatant. Coastal mangroves, for example, have been wiped out for "development projects" such as port facilities or industrial parks, while the island's central forest has been cleared to make way for water reservoirs, leaving only a modicum of protected nature reserves and patches of manicured parks that have been installed as an antidote to rapidly vanishing flora. Accordingly, the almost complete annihilation of wilderness and original forests, along with the demolition of entire historical areas deemed "unsafe," are still by and large considered insignificant side effects of the city-state's particular model of development. And this very temperament in turn can be credited to the national mantra of "land scarcity" that has served time and again as political justification for Singapore's disciplinarian mode of governance. While it is true that land here is limited, this circumstance is presented in governmental rhetoric as an absolute condition of growth, and to dispute said logic is to oppose Singapore's very right to exist, which for so many has proven to be an untenable political rallying cry or credible rival agenda. Economic development is placed above any other matter, and the island's cultural and historical heritage has carried little weight in stemming the tide of ongoing development, save for the few iconic buildings and areas that stand as scant reminders of the

A MODERNIST DREAM TO CREATE NEW LAND THAT CAN BE INSCRIBED WITH NEW STORIES (SOURCE: LINO MOSER AND GABRIELA SCHÄR, ETH ARCHITECTURE OF TERRITORY, 2013)

unrelenting course of development. Although still relevant to collective memory and social identity, older buildings or sacred spaces do not usually garner any sustained reverence from government officials. In fact, such sentiments are most often ridiculed as overly nostalgic and out of touch with the directives of progress. A case in point was in 1966, when Lim Kim San, first chairman of the Housing & Development Board, rhetorically asked a group of elderly citizens who had assembled to oppose the demolition of the Tiong Bahru cemetery, "Do you want me to look after your dead grandparents or do you want me to look after your grandchildren?"—a rather scornful remark epitomizing the state's general stance toward such concerns that in sum still tend to be disregarded as trivial and backward, even unpatriotic.[8] Religious issues are dealt with in a similar disdainful manner, with temples wantonly relocated to industrial areas in order to clear the way for new development, the rationale again being that the nation's economic progress is of prime importance and thus supersedes any other matter at hand. Therefore, governing in Singapore is, in principle and practice, a pragmatic and secular task devoted to economic prosperity above all.

SPIRITUAL SPACES AS A PARALLEL UNIVERSE

Despite Singapore's signature technocratic and pragmatic stature, there is another spiritual, superstitious, and supernatural side to the island nation. For instance, the HDB carefully manages all public expressions of religious faith and incorporates spaces of worship into planning schemes to uphold moral values (i.e., churches, mosques, temples).[9] Despite such state provisions, older beliefs and traditions (e.g., feng shui principles, shrines, festivals, rituals) are customarily honored in many routines of everyday life. It is true that the Chinese syncretic belief system—rich in rituals and spiritual guidelines—is more respected and practiced by the elderly, including ancestor worship and paying tribute to the dead, which are essential rites of both Confucianism and Taoism.[10] Nevertheless, altars and makeshift shrines are a ubiquitous sight in many shops, at home entrances, in hawker centers and fresh meat and fish markets across the island.[11]

If urban planning schemes are devised to create a harmonious, multicultural society, lives in Singapore are drawn into parallel universes by spiritual beliefs. Since its independence, the city-state has witnessed dramatic transformations in terms of religious practices, especially due to the rapid spread of evangelical Christianity, (i.e., the rise of "mega churches" such as the City Harvest Church).[12] However, many Singaporeans, in particular those of ethnic Chinese origin, aspire to some form of spiritual redemption by participating in rituals, consulting mediums, hearing divinations at temples, giving alms and offerings, attending sacramental operas, or participating in pilgrimages. Such activities frequently occur beyond sanctioned public realms and, as a rule, remain imperceptible to tourists or expats or even city planners, yet constitute a widespread phenomenon that is at odds with the sleek, cultivated image of the global city.[13]

All the same, concerted efforts to make uncanny phenomena more perceptible do indeed create peculiar spatial circumstances, and in so doing, give rise to a spectral urban geography, insofar as religious or spiritual activities here strive to spatially represent non-bodied spirits for all to experience and thus make them a palpable part of everyday city life.[14] For instance, numerous informal sacred spaces can be found in HDB estates, where a faction of the Singaporean Chinese religious leadership—comprised of thousands of "spirit mediums"—actually subverts and resists the functionalist policies of the state by turning apartments or ground floors of public housing into provisional ritual spaces for religious activities.[15] While it is said that these mediums can connect to the other world regardless of their physical location, Singapore's internal security agency does all that it can to closely monitor and clamp down on what the PAP considers "religious excess." This is because private beliefs in an alternative reality run counter to the social development vision endorsed by authorities and, as divergent, heretical visions, are considered a potential threat to the city's social order.[16]

WHEN THE GATES OF HELL ARE OPEN

Singaporeans claim that their city is one of the world's most haunted.[17] According to cultural legend, spirits are an ever-present phenomenon and there is one event in particular that perpetuates the belief in ghosts and their pervasiveness on the island: the Hungry Ghost Festival. A month-long spiritual period celebrated and observed mostly by ethnic Chinese communities, the Hungry Ghost Festival takes place during the seventh month of the lunar calendar (usually around mid-August), when the "gates of hell" are said to be open. It is alleged that during this time ancestral spirits are released from the netherworld to roam the earth freely. And during their "journey of purgatory," they of course need sufficient sustenance, entertainment, and money, all of which is courteously offered by individuals as well as social groups. The offering of food and affiliated burning of incense, meant to appease one's ancestors and other wandering spirits, is an important and prevalent ritual practiced outdoors in public spaces throughout the city. Food and gifts are arranged on small makeshift altars (i.e., simple tables, cardboard plates) placed along the roadside or at strategic transitory points like staircases. This collective act of reclaiming and appropriating public space for the sake of spiritual practices is hard to miss. For the positioning of these miniature altars is never random and it is argued that these "uncanny transactions" take place particularly at points of rapid spatial and social change: construction sites, infrastructure junctures, and other significant nodes of a thriving speculative economy.[18]

Joss paper, replica paper money collectively known as *kim zua* or "hell money," is also burned at these altars or in specifically designated incense-burning drums provided by authorities. Large metal containers also allow for burning bigger items; paper servants, paper villas, paper computers, paper clothes, and paper cars are set ablaze, and in this way are sent to the ancestral spirits for them to make use of in the netherworld. At night, flickering red flames rise high above the heads of faithful enthusiasts as the dancing light of the bonfire reflects on nearby facades; the streets come alive and the crowd seems spellbound by the animated elements performing their purifying ritual in the city-state's hyper-controlled urban environment. The stark contrast between the meter-high flames of sporadic fires and the restrained, clinical atmosphere of the city during Hungry Ghost Festival is a peculiar sight indeed that, as strange

DURING THE HUNGRY GHOST FESTIVAL, SOME HDB ESTATES SET UP A COMMUNAL SPOT WHERE PEOPLE COME TOGETHER TO BURN PAPER MONEY AND LEAVE OFFERINGS FOR ALL SPIRITS (SOURCE: ESTHER LEONG, AUGUST 25, 2017)

as it is, seems to capture the contradictory duality of spatial realities and spiritual unrealities. While the fires at first might evoke a sensation of violent urban riots, these rituals are performed according to well-rehearsed dramaturgies and are in fact meticulously managed via close state monitoring.

According to visual sociologist Terence Heng, these rituals, simultaneously private and public, are considered physical narratives that tell stories of beliefs, values, and identities through markers, so-called "material artifacts that perform an individual's or collective's ethnic identities" as manifested in space.[19] These markers—made in the form of offerings—exist only for a short period and are consumed, burned, or removed once the Hungry Ghost Festival has ended, underscoring the ephemeral and only vaguely comprehensible character of this spatial event. As so many visual signs of presumed ghostly presences, the array of objects establishes a specific connection between individuals and a transient space that emerges as a mental geography of sorts, liberated from built realities.

Another element of the festival is the boisterous performance of live songs, the so-called *getai*, which typically occurs only in residential areas. These impromptu performances usually take place on temporary stages next to hawker centers,

CEREMONIES IN THE STREET DURING THE HUNGRY GHOST FESTIVAL:
BACKSTAGE AT A *GETAI* THEATER (LEFT), BURNING OF HELL MONEY (MIDDLE AND RIGHT)
(SOURCES: PHILLIP ALDRUP, AUGUST 2011 AND ALEXA RADU, SEPTEMBER 9, 2017)

in open ground-floor spaces, or in parking lots of the HDB estates, all with glamorous set designs, bright decorations, loud music, and are often accompanied by traditional plays performed in front of a seated audience by semi-professional actors wearing elaborate costumes and colorful make-up. It is customary to leave the first row of seats empty, leaving them available for wandering ghosts. While the offerings are often intended to ensure good luck for the remainder of the year, a complete set of rules and countless moral guidelines are in place to protect devout Singaporeans from ghostly misdeeds during the Hungry Ghost Festival. Believers are advised, for instance, not to whistle alone at night, not to spit on a tree, and to restrain themselves from being overly emotional. In recent years, individuals and groups have even launched social media campaigns to address youth and expatriates with helpful tips and so-called "boos and don'ts" for the festival.[20]

"UTTER RUBBISH!"—GHOSTS AND THE REAL ESTATE MARKET

It would be a gross understatement to say that Singapore's inhabitants are superstitious. During the Hungry Ghost Festival, apprehensive Singaporeans are particularly wary of buying new apartments, for the desired property may very well be haunted by roving spirits. Renovation work or house moves during this time are considered ill-fated as well and are therefore commonly avoided. However, real estate transactions during the seventh calendar month are steady and there is no significant decrease in sales. This is perhaps because non-superstitious buyers often take advantage of low housing demand during the Hungry Ghost Festival, resulting in lower prices and discounts of up to 10 per cent compared to other months of the year.[21] Lee Kuan Yew's take on this matter is clear: "Utter rubbish! Utter rubbish! I'm a pragmatic, practical fellow. I do not believe in horoscopes. I do not believe in feng shui. And I'm not superstitious about numbers. But if you have a house [...] with disadvantaged feng shui and numbers, when you buy it, you must consider that when you resell. So again it's a practical consideration. [...] if I buy that, I must get a low price because when I sell it I will get a low price."[22]

In Hong Kong, start-ups capitalize on the cultural fear among Chinese residents about living in haunted spaces and are more than eager to hustle so called "stigmatized properties" to millennial expats.[23] In Japan, Mr Oshima's already legendary, extensive map of haunted homes has proven to be a veritable nightmare for landlords.[24] Singapore's stigmatized properties are beginning to be mapped online as well, a most welcome facilitator of potentially cheaper real estate on the high-priced island. Needless to say, real estate developers and property brokers remain wary of superstitious clients and are openly dismissive of proliferating ghost stories.[25] Unsurprisingly, exorcism and so-called "deceased appeasement" have become lucrative for the city's enterprising ghostbusters, insofar as the price for coaxing a resident spirit to move out of a unit can run well into the thousands of Singapore dollars.[26] Beside the

COMBINED REAL ESTATE AND GHOST MAP FOR HONG KONG (SOURCE: SPACIOUS.HK, 2018)

periodic visit of ghosts from the netherworld, more permanent apparitions have been reported in some locations around the island. The *pontianaks*—a name one should not pronounce—the restless souls of the massacred, the *toyols*, the twisted spirit of small children who passed away before birth, the banana spirits or the warrior ghosts, allegedly dwelling in banyan trees, are all said to haunt remote isles in the Singapore straits literally called "Ghost Island,"[27] water ponds, or even subway trains.

The suspected presence of ghosts, thought to mirror the existence of another world, is expressed directly in the belief that the spaces of this world which they occupy are haunted, with some going so far as to claim that the entire island of Singapore is haunted as well. In fact, even when spaces have been purified, as it were, of any previous traces of human activity (i.e., graves, houses), the superstition remains, a testimony to the resilience of memory and spirituality amidst fast-paced development. As urban growth devours cemeteries, schoolyards, residential blocks, and older buildings deemed an obstacle to Singapore's ongoing modernization, the ghosts inhabiting them persist, lingering in people's memory and creeping into new constructions as if to perpetuate the island's lore. Michel de Certeau

EXORCISM RITUALS IN SINGAPORE
(SOURCE: RAZOR TV, 2018)

claimed in *The Practice of Everyday Life* that "There is no place that is not haunted by many different spirits hidden there in silence, spirits one can 'invoke' or not."[28] Singaporeans continue to invoke and honor ancestral spirits, seeking a continuous, unbroken bond between living and dead family members, while primarily asking them for mercy, financial success, guidance and protection, but perhaps also to cope with the excessive rationality that prevails on their island and to retain something of a long-gone past. Spirits are said to exist in the oddest of places. The shopping malls of Orchard Road, for example, would seem to be devoid of spirituality, given over as such temples of consumption are to satisfying consumer temptations. Yet, the Gucci boutique shop hides an altar in one of its glass cabinets, hidden so as to not to disturb the sleek aesthetic of modernity, but nevertheless dutifully installed in deference to the store's occupant spirits.

GHOST STORIES AS ECHOES AND COUNTER-FANTASIES

Singapore's history is infused with ghost stories. In 1819, soon after Singapore was established as a modern-day British trading

LUXURY BUDDHIST ALTAR SET USED IN SHOPS (SOURCE: GLOBAL RAKUTEN MARKET, 2018)
PULAU HANTU (MALAY FOR "GHOST ISLAND") IS A SMALL ISLAND LOCATED IN THE STRAITS OF SINGAPORE, JUST OFF THE COAST OF SINGAPORE ISLAND (SOURCE: THEFINDER.COM.SG, 2018)

outpost, Sir Stamford Raffles called for an excursion to climb Fort Canning Hill, then called Bukit Larangan, Malay for "The Forbidden Hill." When the men of the Temenggong (the local "chief of public security") warned him, "None of us have the courage to go up that hill because there are many ghosts on it. Every day one can hear on it sounds as from hundreds of men. Sometimes one hears the sound of heavy drums and of people shouting," Raffles was reported to have scoffed, saying, "I should like to see your ghosts."[29] The story does not mention if he actually met any. But the constant influx of immigrants certainly brought to the island an abundance of beliefs and supernatural traditions from abroad: stories of *yau gwee* ("hungry ghosts" in Hokkien) from China, *hantu* (ghosts in Malay) from the Malay archipelago, *mohini* (vengeful female spirits) from India, as well *jinn* ("spirits") from the Arab world. And these diverse beliefs soon took root in local cultural lore.

While the moral codes transported via stories seem to be timeless, the ways in which they are told have changed tremendously. Evolving over time from oral folklore to a mass entertainment medium, ghost stories today constitute a vital part of Singapore's popular culture. Epic movies such as B. Narayan Rao's *Dendam Pontianak* (1957) or best-selling book series such as *The Almost Complete Collection of True Singaporean Ghost Stories* by Russell Lee are proof of this enduring heritage.[30] Besides classic media formats, the web and social networks have further increased the spread of ghost stories and spiritual content in recent years, detaching them from their particular origin. Today, applications for smartphones that convey religious messages complement online forums and blogs discussing haunted places around the city, giving such stories a life on their own. Domestic ghost-hunters have even developed online guides to the island's allegedly most haunted spots. It is conceivable that ghost stories in this context manifest a counter-fantasy to the progressive, orderly, yet sterile neighborhoods and to the erudite, prosperous, but overly materialistic communities that Singapore has nurtured over recent decades. The irrationality of mystical belief and widespread reception of ghost stories are durable echoes of the sanitized city-state. A question arises as to whether the ghost stories provide a diversion or form of escape from the hyper-rational reality confronted by the majority of Singaporeans. Perhaps this is the case, but certain recent events have either spurred on or inhibited the belief in haunted buildings. The 1997 financial crisis in Asia, for instance, left many buildings unfinished or abandoned throughout the Singapore region (i.e., Batam Island, Johor Bahru). And there is no better place for wandering ghosts in search of a home, so it goes, than a deserted building that, because uninhabited, is no longer subject to the ever-watchful eye of the authorities. For this very reason, those desolate properties, devoid of life and human activity, are often suspected of being haunted, and so are featured in spectral narratives in which recurring architectural details like grating doors or broken windows serve as a kind of dramaturgic shorthand. Not only signaling absence and lack of maintenance in a strictly functional sense, these material symbols indicate for

MARIA MENADO AS THE PONTIANAK, A FEMALE VAMPIRE FROM MALAY MYTHOLOGY, IN *DENDAM PONTIANAK*, DIRECTED BY B. NARAYAN RAO AND PRODUCED BY CATHAY-KERIS FILMS, 1957

so many the all-too-likely presence of ghosts, which in Singapore is by now a common, matter-of-fact prospect. The close company of spirits is widely accepted as commonplace, at once natural and supernatural. However, this familiarity with and proximity of the netherworld—facilitated by the multitude of makeshift altars and numerous temples—is complemented by a pronounced reservation about ghost stories. Some are reluctant to talk about the issue, as if even the mention of such accounts is enough to bring on personal misfortune. And this very reservation gets translated directly into space as well. In the collective subconscious, haunted spaces should above all be avoided, and if transgressed at all, it is usually only by adventurous teenagers, outsiders, and eccentrics.

CLOSING REMARKS

Each of the spaces discussed and presented in this book's heterogeneous collection are taken to be haunted, regardless of their location, status, or scale. A host of reasons justify this culturally ingrained conviction, some more tangible or legitimate than others. Whether as sites of gruesome murders and fatal accidents, as former battlegrounds and cemeteries, or as contested spaces and morally charged landscapes, the validity of claims is of little importance in the end. Despite the assertions made, any ghost story is first and foremost based on hearsay. What is of prime relevance is the social presence of ghosts, which serves to convey memories. Buildings might be demolished and cemeteries leveled, yet the rumors of a haunted site remain lodged in the collective imaginary. In a country so strictly controlled and with so little space for spontaneity, the lingering presence of supernatural forces is perhaps indicative of a low-lying cultural opposition of sorts. Do these mystical rituals and their material fallout signal latent discontent and concealed social dysfunction? Could it be that the alleged habitation of the built environment by spirits gestures at some innate resistance mechanism devised by humans against the loss of memory, disappearance of reference points, and eroding sense of belonging when faced with indiscriminate planning directives and fast-tracked urban development? Whatever the answers may be, Singapore stands as a built and lived paradox, rationally planned and socially engineered as a model city-state, and at the same time cast as a haunted island said to be the province of wandering spirits in search of a suitable earthly abode. And as these competing parallel narratives continue to make their respective claims on people and space, Singapore's gung-ho capitalist spirit in this world is offset almost imperceptibly by the nation's purported host of otherworldly spirits.

1 World Economic Outlook Database, April 12, 2017, International Monetary Fund.

2 Brian G. Field, "The Morphology of Planning in an Urban Laboratory," *Property Management* 17, 2 (1999).

3 Lee Kuan Yew, interview, *The Straits Times*, March 25, 1985.

4 Christopher Tremewan, *The Political Economy of Social Control in Singapore*, St Antony's Series (New York: St Martin's Press, 1994).

5 This only concerns built-to-order sales but not re-sales.

6 Milica Topalovic et al., *Constructed Land—Singapore 1924–2012*, exhibition at 2014 International Architecture Biennale Rotterdam.

7 Ibid; Lim Yi Yong. *SEA STATE*, exhibition at 2015 Venice Biennale.

8 Asad Latif and Lim Kim San, *A Builder of Singapore* (Singapore: Institute of Southeast Asian Studies, 2009), 80.

9 Vineeta Sinha, "Marking Spaces as 'Sacred': Infusing Singapore's Urban Landscape with Sacrality," *International Sociology* 31 (2016).

10 See Ah Eng Lai, *Religious Diversity in Singapore*, Iseas E-Books (Singapore: Institute of Policy Studies & Lee Kuan Yew School of Public Policy, 2008).

11 Randy Chan and Jolene Lee, "Hawker Centres: Siting/Sighting Singapore's Food Heritage," in *Public Space in Urban Asia*, edited by William S.W. Lim (Singapore: World Scientific Publishing Co. Pte. Ltd., 2014).

12 Kenneth Dean, "Parallel Universes: Chinese Temple Networks in Singapore, or What Is Missing in the Singapore Model?" in *Handbook of Religion and the Asian City: Aspiration and Urbanization in the Twenty-First Century*, edited by Peter van der Veer (Oakland: University of California Press, 2015).

13 Ibid.

14 David Parkin, "Ritual as Spatial Direction and Bodily Division," in *Understanding Rituals*, edited by Daniel de Coppet (London: Routledge, 1992).

15 Terence Heng, "Making 'Unofficial' Sacred Space: Spirit Mediums and House Temples in Singapore," in *Geographical Review*, 106, 2 (2016).

16 Dean (2015).

17 Joshua Comaroff, "The Garden of Ghosts: Landscape and Recollection in Singapore," lecture at the University of Technology Sydney, May 11, 2017.

18 Ibid.

19 Terence Heng, "Hungry Ghosts in Urban Spaces: A Visual Study of Aesthetic Markers and Material Anchoring," in *Visual Communication*, 13, 2 (2014), 147–162.

20 "Here are all the 5 posters of Singa the Courtesy Ghost Boos and Don'ts", Mothership Singapore, mothership.sg/2014/08/here-are-all-the-5-posters-of-singa-the-courtesy-ghosts-boos-and-donts

21 "The 'Hungry Ghost Month' Effect on Housing," Asia One (September 2, 2015): online at www.asiaone.com/business/hungry-ghost-month-effect-housing (accessed June 18, 2018).

22 Lee Kuan Yew, *Hard Truths to Keep Singapore Going* (Singapore: Straits Times Press, 2011).

23 "This Hong Kong Tech Startup Is Hustling Haunted Apartments to Millennial Expats," Motherboard (Vice) (September 8, 2016): online at mother-board.vice.com/en_us/article/vv7ykj/hong-kongs-property-ghost-hunters (accessed June 18, 2018).

24 "Map of 'Haunted' Homes Is Landlords' Nightmare in Japan," *Wall Street Journal* (October 30, 2014): online at wsj.com/articles/map-of-haunted-homes-is-landlords-nightmare-in-japan-1414687248 (accessed August 10, 2018). "Stigmatized Property Map," Oshima Land (2005–2018): online at oshimaland.com (accessed August 10, 2018). In Japan, landlords are obliged by law to indicate to possible tenants or buyers whether their property is stigmatized or not (e.g., because of a murder case, death).

25 Laura Ruggeri, "The Poetics of Urban Inscription: from Metaphorical Cognition to Counter-representation," in *Critical Architecture*, edited by Jane Rendell, Mark Dorrian, Jonathan Hill and Murray Fraser (London: Routledge, 2008).

26 "Exorcism, Singapore Style," Things Asian (April 23, 2011): online at thingsasian.com/story/exorcism-singapore-style (accessed August 10, 2018).

27 Legend has it that two Malay warriors once dueled and died here, and they were both transformed into small islands for their ghosts to live on them. The small island was called Pulau Hantu Kecil, and the other, bigger one, was called Pulau Hantu Besar.

28 Michel de Certeau, *The Practice of Everyday Life* (Berkeley: University of California Press, 1984), 108.

29 Abdullah Abdul Kadir, *The Hikayat Abdullah* (Kuala Lumpur: The Malaysian Branch of the Royal Asiatic Society, 2009), 146. Abdullah claims that Colonel William Farquhar organized the expedition; later historians established that it was almost certainly Raffles.

30 See "True Singaporean Ghost Stories," Flame of the Forest (2017): online at flameoftheforest.com/books/russell-lee/ (accessed August 10, 2018).

PHOTO ESSAY CAPTIONS

Photography by Philipp Aldrup

COLOPHON

Marcel Jäggi, Charlotte Malterre-Barthes
SOME HAUNTED SPACES IN SINGAPORE

Editing: Marcel Jäggi, Charlotte Malterre-Barthes, Patrick Frey, Andreas Koller
Texts: Lilian Chee, Charles Goh, Marcel Jäggi, Denise L., Charlotte Malterre-Barthes, Mary-Ann Ray, Jones Tang
Copyediting: Louise Stein, Cary Siress
Proofreading: Jacob Blandy

Photo credits: Philipp Aldrup, Marcel Jäggi, Charlotte Malterre-Barthes, Oliver Vogler

Book design: Maximage
Printed and bound by Musumeci S.p.A., Quart (Aosta)
Papers: Magno Gloss 100 g/m², Profibulk 1.1 100 g/m², Sirio Color Nero 115 g/m²
Cover: Sirio Color Nero 290 g/m²
Typefaces: Antique, François Rappo
Rhymes, Jakub Samek

First edition: Edition Patrick Frey, 2018
Print run: 800 copies
ISBN 978-3-906803-71-5
Printed in Italy

Edition Patrick Frey
Limmatstrasse 268
CH-8005 Zürich
www.editionpatrickfrey.com
mail@editionpatrickfrey.ch

ACKNOWLEDGEMENTS

This work would not have been possible without the invaluable contributions and hard work of the following individuals, to whom we are extremly grateful for joining our "ghost" team: Philipp Aldrup (photo essay), Diego Bettinaglio (maps), Omar Khaledi (cardboard models), Nicole Köhler (cardboard models), Mohamed Ossama Gabrallah (3D models), Oliver Vogler (model photography).

The authors would also like to thank: Diana Alvarez Marin, Marc Angélil, Lilian Chee, Edition Patrick Frey, ETH Zurich, Future Cities Laboratory Singapore, Charles Goh, Kaspar Helfrich, Alex Lehnerer, Denise L., OOS Architekten, Raffael Petrovic, Tracy Phillips, pool Architekten, Mary-Ann Ray, Cary Siress, Lorenzo Stieger, Jones Tang, the taxi drivers of Singapore, Petra Tomljanovic, Milica Topalovic, U5, Vivian Wang.

Marcel Jäggi would like to thank: Goda Budvytyte, Stephen Cairns, Christina Chua, Thomas Friberg, Ghim Moh Market and Hawker Center, Thomas Hildebrand, Janaïna Huber, Adam Jasper Smith, Lee Kah Wee, Rahmat "Bobbie" Kurniawan, Kenny Leck, Benjamin Leclair-Pacquet, Charles Lim, Reto Müller, Fabian Niklaus, Sascha Roesler, Rafael Ruprecht, Michelle Schwarzenbach, Mriz Sidah, Dean Swan, Alvin Tan, Dennis Tan, Valerie Wee, Nicole Yau, Peter, Ursula Jäggi-Zurbrügg.

Charlotte Malterre-Barthes would like to thank: Lorenz Bürgi, Kenneth Chong, Deborah Chung, Rohit Gandhi, Gautam Gangaram, Stefan Graber, Norman Hack, Kurien Kalarickal, Victor Koh, Marija Maric, Priyanka Mirchandandi, Prapti Rao, Pranav Sethaputra, Jayartnam "Paalan" Theyvapaalan, Tiong Bahru Bakery, Justin Yeoh.

DISTRIBUTION

Switzerland
AVA Verlagsauslieferung
CH—Affoltern am Albis
ava.ch

Germany, Austria
GVA Gemeinsame Verlagsauslieferung
D—Göttingen
gva-verlage.de

France, Luxembourg, Belgium
Les presses du réel
F—Dijon
lespressesdureel.com

United Kingdom
Antenne Books
GB—London
antennebooks.com

United States
ARTBOOK/D.A.P.
USA—New York
artbook.com

Japan
twelvebooks
JP—Tokyo
twelve-books.com

Australia, New Zealand
Perimeter Distribution
AU—Melbourne
perimeterdistribution.com

Other countries
Edition Patrick Frey
CH—Zürich
editionpatrickfrey.com